"This is as c[illegible] its that you will find. Now, parents [illegible] learning opportunities to raise respe[illegible]."

—G[illegible] counselor at Zemmer Jr. High, Lapeer, Michigan

"*Parenting with Love and Logic* is an essential component for our students, parents, and teachers. For the last fourteen years, thousands of families in our school district have been positively impacted by love and logic principles."

—LEONARD R. REZMIERSKI, PhD, superintendent of Northville Public Schools

"*Parenting with Love and Logic* is a MUST for every parent in America! This is the most useful book I've ever read. This stuff really works! My kids use this stuff on me, their peers, and their teachers! That's how I know it really works!"

—LORYNDA SAMPSON, Colorado Teacher of the Year, 2003

"For almost twenty years, I have been delighted to share the powerful, yet simple wisdom of Jim Fay and Foster Cline with my counseling clients. The principles in *Parenting with Love and Logic* are practical, proven techniques that keep parents on track to raising responsible, loving, confident children."

—CAROL R. COLE, PhD, LMFT

"*Parenting with Love and Logic* is a terrific book for parents that provides important concepts and practical solutions to help children become emotionally, socially, and morally healthy."

—TERRY M. LEVY, PhD, codirector of Evergreen Psychotherapy Center; coauthor of *Attachment, Trauma and Healing*

GWYN BODDY

Parenting with Love and Logic

Teaching Children Responsibility

UPDATED AND EXPANDED EDITION

Foster Cline, MD and Jim Fay

NAVPRESS

NAVPRESS

NavPress is the publishing ministry of The Navigators, an international Christian organization and leader in personal spiritual development. NavPress is committed to helping people grow spiritually and enjoy lives of meaning and hope through personal and group resources that are biblically rooted, culturally relevant, and highly practical.

For a free catalog go to www.NavPress.com
or call 1.800.366.7788 in the United States or 1.800.839.4769 in Canada.

ISBN-13: 978-1-61747-177-3

Cover design by: Kirk DuPonce, DogEaredDesign.com
Cover photo by: Jupiter Images and Getty Images
Creative Team: Terry Behimer, Cara Iverson, Darla Hightower, Arvid Wallen, Laura Spray

First edition text was written by Tom Raabe.
Second edition prepared by Rick Killian, Killian Creative, Boulder, Colorado, www.killiancreative.com

Library of Congress Cataloging-in-Publication Data

Cline, Foster.
Parenting with love and logic : teaching children responsibility / Foster Cline and Jim Fay.-- Updated and expanded ed.
p. cm.
Includes bibliographical references and index.
ISBN 1-57683-954-0
1. Parent and child. 2. Parenting. 3. Responsibility in children. I. Fay, Jim. II. Title.
HQ755.85.C58 2006
649'.64--dc22

2005037527

Printed in the United States of America

1 2 3 4 5 6 7 / 15 14 13 12 11

To all the parents and children (including our own!)
who were my teachers, and to my wife, Hermie, who gave support.

—Foster

To my wife, Shirley,
whose love, support, and wisdom have always been
a source of motivation and strength.

—Jim

Contents

Foreword to the Second Edition

We have been gratified to see the response that the world has given *Parenting with Love and Logic* and *Parenting Teens with Love and Logic.* Since these books were first published in 1990 and 1992, they have had twenty-six and seventeen printings respectively and have been translated into eight languages. Parents on six continents—all except Antarctica—have effectively embraced Love and Logic concepts. During these years since the first edition, we have happily collected success stories of parents who excitedly and proudly told us of raising their children with choices, consequences, and empathy, as taught in *Parenting with Love and Logic.*

While sales have continued to increase, it is apparent that the world has changed in many ways since the books were written. In those days, there was no instant messaging, no talking to strangers in chat rooms, no computer games. Toddlers didn't own plastic toys that took turns spouting off the alphabet, tutoring children on naming colors, and helping them learn to spell. Yet no matter the generation, good parenting boils down to loving and effective parent-child relationships and communication that engender respect and self-discipline.

Our goal in this second edition has not changed, but we have added information on how parents can specifically handle the new challenges our children face. This new information includes real-life examples of effective communication between parents and their kids.

We thank the parents who have told us how the principles here have helped them raise children who are equipped to make good decisions and who are loving, responsible, and fun to be around. We also thank those who have given us ideas and suggestions, some of which have been included in this edition.

Foster Cline and Jim Fay
March 2006

Introduction

For hundreds of years, rookie parents learned the fine points of child rearing by example: They took the techniques their parents had used on them and applied them to their own children. Today this approach is more apt to bomb than boom.

Many of us, when we meet failure in parenting, throw up our hands in frustration and say, "I can't understand it. It worked for my dad!" Yes, it did. But things have changed. The human rights revolution, the communication explosion, the Internet, cell phones, changes in the nuclear family—these and many other factors have radically changed how our children view life. Kids are forced to grow up quicker these days, so they need to learn sooner how to cope with the tremendous challenges and pressures of contemporary life. The impact of rising divorce rates, single parents raising kids, blended families, and other changes in the family has been dramatic. Parents must learn to use different techniques with kids who live in today's complex, rapidly changing world.

That's where Parenting with Love and Logic comes in. Why the terms *love* and *logic*? Effective parenting centers around love: love that is not permissive, love that doesn't tolerate disrespect, but also love that is powerful enough to allow kids to make mistakes and permit them to live with the consequences of those mistakes. Most mistakes do have logical consequences. And those consequences, when accompanied by empathy—our compassionate understanding of the child's disappointment, frustration, and pain—hit home with mind-changing power.

This book is written in two parts. In the first, we will lay out our concepts on parenting in general terms, centering on building self-concept, separating problems, neutralizing anger and arguments, using thinking words and enforceable statements, offering choices, and locking in our empathy before our kids face the consequences of their mistakes. These are the building blocks of effective parenting. Part 1 also contains extra tidbits of information—"Love and Logic Tips"—which add flesh to the bone of many Love and Logic principles.

In the second part, we get practical. The forty-eight Love and Logic pearls offer everyday strategies for dealing with problems most parents will face during the first twelve or so years of their children's lives. These pearls build on the general ideas developed in the first half of the book and should be used only after the first part has been read and understood.

Parenting with Love and Logic is not a foolproof system that works every time. No system can promise that. But it *is* a system that has a strong chance of working in most situations. Although Love and Logic is not a comprehensive system, it is a complete system. That is, although we have not written a thick tome containing every detail of parent-child relationship, how best to handle almost every issue can be gleaned from these pages. Parents will find success using the Love and Logic attitude. Once the attitude is mastered, handling most problems becomes second nature, even when a particular problem has not been explored. Our approach is more of an attitude that will allow our children to grow in maturity as they grow in years. It will teach them to think, to decide, and to live with their decisions. In short, it will teach them responsibility, and that's what parenting is all about. If we can teach our kids responsibility, we've accomplished a great portion of our parental task.

The Bible provides insight on many parenting issues. Much of what this book teaches is summarized beautifully in a familiar Old Testament proverb:

> Train children in the right way,
> and when old, they will not stray. (Proverbs 22:6)

What greater gift can parents give their children than the opportunity for a joyful, productive, and responsible adult life? We believe that the principles of *Parenting with Love and Logic* will help achieve that result.

Part 1

The Love and Logic Parent

1

Parenting: Joy or Nightmare?

A wise child loves discipline,
but a scoffer does not listen to rebuke.
Proverbs 13:1

A mother and father stand outside of a restaurant in the rain asking their three-year-old, Chloe, to get in the car so the family can go home. Chloe refuses. Her parents spend the next fifteen minutes begging and pleading with her to do it on her own. At one point, the father gets down on his knees in the puddles, trying to reason her into the car. She finally complies, but only after her parents agree to buy her a soda on the way home. If they have to use a soda to buy her off at three, what will they be facing when she reaches sixteen?

Jim sits in the airport awaiting a flight, watching as a mother gives at least eighty different demands to her three-year-old boy over the course of an hour without ever enforcing one of them:

"Come back here, Logan!"

"Don't go over there, Logan!"

"You better listen to me, Logan, or else!"

"I mean it, Logan!"

"Don't run, Logan!"

"Come back here so you don't get hurt, Logan!"

Logan eventually finds his way to where Jim is seated. The toddler smiles at him while ignoring his mother. The mother yells, "Logan, you get away from that man! You get over here this instant!"

Jim smiles down at Logan and asks, "Hey, Logan, what is your mom going to do if you don't get over there?"

He looks up and grins. "She not goin' to do nothin'." And then his eyes twinkle and his grin becomes wider.

It turns out he is right. She finally comes apologizing. "I'm sorry he's bothering you, but you know how three-year-olds are. They just won't listen to one thing you tell them."

On a Saturday at a local supermarket, two boys—ages five and seven—have declared war. Like guerrillas on a raiding party, they sneak from aisle to aisle, hiding behind displays and squeaking their tennies on the tile floor. Then suddenly a crash—the result of a game of "shopping cart chicken"—pierces the otherwise calming background Muzak.

The mother, having lost sight of this self-appointed commando unit, abandons her half-filled cart. As she rounds a corner, her screams turn the heads of other shoppers: "Don't get lost!" "Don't touch that!" "*You*—get over here!" She races for the boys, and as she's about to grab two sweaty necks, they turn to Tactic B: "the split up," a twenty-first-century version of "divide and conquer." Now she must run in two directions at once to shout at them. Wheezing with exertion, she corrals the younger one, who just blitzed the cereal section, leaving a trail of boxes. But when she returns him to her cart, the older boy is gone. She locates him in produce, rolling seedless grapes like marbles across the floor.

After scooping up Boy Number Two and carrying him back, you guessed it, she finds that Boy Number One has disappeared. Mom sprints from her cart once more. Finally, after she threatens murder and the pawning of their Nintendo game system, the boys are gathered.

But the battle's not over. Tactic C follows: the "fill the cart when Mom's not looking" game. Soon M&Ms, Oreos, vanilla wafers, and jumbo Snickers bars are piled high. Mom races back and forth reshelving the treats. Then come boyish smirks and another round of threats from Mom: "Don't do that!" "I'm going to slap your hands!" And in a cry of desperation: "You're never going to leave the house again for the rest of your lives!"

Frazzled, harried, and broken, Mom finally surrenders and buys off her precious flesh and blood with candy bars—a cease-fire that guarantees enough peace to finish her rounds.

Are We Having Fun Yet?

Ah, yes, parenting—the joys, the rewards. We become parents with optimism oozing from every pore. During late-night feedings and sickening diaper changes, we know we are laying the groundwork for a lifelong relationship that will bless us when our hair turns gray or disappears. We look forward to times of tenderness and times of love, shared joys and shared disappointments, hugs and encouragement, words of comfort, and soul-filled conversations.

But the joys of parenting were far from the minds of the parents in the previous stories. No freshly scrubbed cherubs flitted through their lives, hanging on every soft word dropping from Mommy's or Daddy's lips. Where was that gratifying, loving, personal relationship between parent and child? The sublime joys of parenting were obliterated by a more immediate concern: survival.

This was parenting, the nightmare.

Scenes like these happen to the best of us. When they do, we may want to throw our hands in the air and scream, "Kids! Are they worth the pain?" Sometimes kids can be a bigger hassle than a house with one shower. When we think of the enormous love we pump into our children's lives and then the sassy, disobedient, unappreciative behavior we receive in return, we can get pretty burned out on the whole process. Besides riddling our lives with day-to-day hassles, kids present us with perhaps the greatest challenge of our adulthood: raising our children to be responsible adults.

Through the miracle of birth, we are given a tiny, defenseless babe totally dependent on us for every physical need. We have a mere eighteen years at most to ready that suckling for a world that can be cruel and heartless. That child's success in the real world hinges in large part on the job we do as parents. Just thinking about raising responsible, well-rounded kids sends a sobering shiver of responsibility right up the old parental spine. Many of us have felt queasy after a thought such as this: *If I can't handle a five-year-old in a grocery store, what am I going to do with a fifteen-year-old who seems to have an enormous understanding of sex and is counting the days until he gets a driver's license?*

Putting the Fun Back into Parenting

All is not so bleak. Trust us! There's hope, shining beacon bright, at the end of the tunnel of parental frustration. Parenting doesn't have to be drudgery. Children can grow to be thinking, responsible adults. We can help them do it without living through an eighteen-year horror movie.

Parenting with Love and Logic is all about raising responsible kids. It's a win-win philosophy. Parents win because they love in a healthy way and establish control over their kids without resorting to the anger and threats that encourage rebellious teenage behavior. Kids win because they learn responsibility and the logic of life by solving their own problems. Thus, they acquire the tools for coping with the real world.

Parents and kids can establish a rewarding relationship built on love and trust in the process. What a deal! Parenting with Love and Logic puts the fun back into parenting.

2

Mission Possible: Raising Responsible Kids

Train children in the right way,
and when old, they will not stray.
Proverbs 22:6

All loving parents face essentially the same challenge: raising children who have their heads on straight and will have a good chance to make it in the big world. Every sincere mom and dad strives to attain this goal. We must equip our darling offspring to make the move from total dependence on us to independence, from being controlled by us to controlling themselves.

Let's face it: In this incredibly complex, fast-changing age, responsible kids are the only ones who will be able to handle the real world that awaits them. Life-and-death decisions confront teenagers—and even younger children—at every turn. Many of the temptations of adult life—drugs, Internet pornography, premarital sex, alcohol—are thrown at kids every day. The statistics on teen depression and suicide bear out the seriousness of the parental task. How will our children handle such intense pressures? What choices will they make when faced with these life-and-death decisions? What will they do when we are no longer pouring wise words into their ears? Will merely telling them to be responsible get the job done? These are the questions that should guide the development of our parenting philosophy.

The gravity of the parenting task hit home some years ago when my (Jim's) son, Charlie, was a teenager. Charlie asked to use the family car to go to a party. "It's the party of the year," Charlie said. "Everybody who's anybody will be there."

I trusted Charlie and would have loaned him the car, but I had a speaking engagement that same evening and couldn't oblige. Charlie's mother, Shirley, also had plans of her own for the second car.

"Why don't you hitch a ride with Randy?" I suggested, referring to Charlie's best friend.

Charlie shook his head. "That's okay. I understand. I guess I won't go." Then he went to his room. I knew something was up. This was *the* party of the year, so I talked to Charlie and pried loose some more information. Randy, it seemed, had started drinking at parties, and Charlie decided he'd rather stay home than risk the danger of riding with a friend who was likely to drink and drive.

The night of that party, Randy, plied with booze, drove himself and five passengers off the side of a mountain at eighty miles per hour.

Today, roughly two decades later, Charlie has earned his PhD and is on staff at the Love and Logic Institute. He is now teaching others the same parenting techniques that saved his life. Because he had learned to be a responsible teen, instead of dying that night, he has gone on to help countless others.

Unfortunately, many kids arrive at their challenging and life-threatening teenage years with no clue as to how to make decisions. They "know better" but still try drugs. They ignore good advice from parents and other adults and dabble with sex. Though they have been warned to be cautious, they are still lured into meetings by Internet predators. Why do young people sometimes seem so stupidly self-destructive? The tragic truth is that many of these foolish choices are the first real decisions they have ever made. In childhood, decisions were always made for them by well-meaning parents. We must understand that making good choices is like any other activity: It has to be learned. The teenagers who make the wrong choice on alcohol are probably the same children who never learned how to keep their hands out of the cookie jar.

Parents who take their parenting job seriously want to raise responsible kids—kids who at any age can confront the important decisions of their lives with maturity and good sense. Good parents learn to do what is best for their children. Those little tykes, so innocent and playful at our feet, will someday grow up. We want to do everything humanly possible for our children so that someday they can strut confidently into the real world. And we do it all in the name of love. But love can get us in trouble—not love itself per se, but how we show it. Our noble intentions are often our own worst enemy when it comes to raising responsible kids.

Contrary to popular opinion, many of the worst kids—the most disrespectful and rebellious—often come from homes where they are shown love, but it's just the wrong kind of love.

Ineffective Parenting Styles

Helicopter Parents

Some parents think that love means revolving their lives around their children. They are helicopter parents. They hover over and then rescue their children whenever trouble arises. They're forever running lunches, permission slips, band instruments, and homework assignments to school. They're always pulling their children out of jams. Not a day goes by when they're not protecting little junior from something—usually from a growing experience—he needs or deserves. As soon as their children send up an SOS flare, helicopter parents, who are ready hovering nearby, swoop in and shield the children from teachers, playmates, and other elements that appear hostile.

While today these "loving" parents may feel they are easing their children's path into adulthood, tomorrow the same children will be leaving home and wasting the first eighteen months of their adult life flunking out of college or meandering about "getting their heads together." Such children are unequipped for the challenges of life. Their significant learning opportunities were stolen from them in the name of love.

The irony is that helicopter parents are often viewed by others as model parents. They feel uncomfortable imposing consequences. When they see their children hurting, they hurt too, so they bail them out.

But the real world does not run on the bail-out principle. Traffic tickets, overdue bills, irresponsible people, crippling diseases, taxes—these and other normal events of adult life usually do not disappear because a loving benefactor bails us out. Helicopter parents fail to prepare their kids to meet that kind of world.

The Evolution of the Helicopter Parent: The Turbo-Attack Helicopter Model

At the first writing of this book, the helicopter parents we were used to meeting were relatively harmless compared to the modern-day version. In the midst of the prosperity of the 1990s, a new type emerged that no longer just rescued and defended; instead, they would fly in with guns blazing and missiles locked in to attack anyone who held their child accountable for his or her actions. We have come to call them the "jet-powered turbo-attack mode" of helicopter parents.

These parents are obsessed with the desire to create a perfect world for their kids. This perfect world is one in which their kids never have to face struggle, inconvenience, discomfort, or disappointment. It is a life in which the child can be launched into adulthood with the best of credentials. They look great on paper with all of their high grades, extracurricular activities, awards, and special honors. These kids lead a life where their mistakes are swept under the table. We have often heard helicopter parents say, "It's a competitive world out there and I want my kids to have every advantage. Mistakes they make when they are young should not hold them back later."

These parents, in their zeal to protect their young, swoop down like jet-powered AH-64 Apache attack helicopters on any person or agency they see as a threat to their child's impeccable credentials. Armed with verbal smart bombs, they are quick to blast away at anyone who sets high standards for behavior, morality, or achievement.

Declaring their child a victim is a favorite tactical maneuver, designed to send school personnel or social workers diving into the trenches for protection. Teachers and school administrators become worn down by these parents' constant barrage. It is horribly disappointing to watch kids learn to blame others for their lack of success instead of becoming people who reach goals through effort and determination. I daily hear about the turbo jet-powered helicopter parents who are not satisfied with just protecting their children but even prefer to destroy the infrastructure of the very agencies dedicated to nurturing their children into educated, moral human beings.

The company who hires a helicopter kid won't be intimidated by parental pressure in the face of substandard performance. A perfect image and spotless school transcript are poor substitutes for character and the attitude that achievement comes through struggle and perseverance. Such aggressive protection of their children will simply accomplish the exact opposite of what helicopter parents are trying to achieve.

Drill Sergeant Parents

Other parents are like drill sergeants. These, too, love their children. They feel that the more they bark and the more they control, the better their kids will be in the long run. "These kids will be disciplined," the drill sergeant says. "They'll know how to act right." Indeed, they are constantly *told* what to do.

When drill sergeant parents talk to children, their words are often filled with put-downs and I-told-you-so's. These parents are into power! If children don't do what they're told, drill sergeant parents are going to—doggone it all—*make* them do it.

Kids of drill sergeant parents, when given the chance to think for themselves, often make horrendous decisions—to the complete consternation and disappointment of their parents. But it makes sense. These kids are rookies in the world of decision making. They've never had to think—the drill sergeant took care of that. The kids have been ordered around all their lives. They're as dependent on their parents as the kids of helicopter parents.

In addition, when the children of drill sergeant parents reach their teen years, they are even more susceptible to peer pressure than most other teens. Why? Because, as children, when the costs of mistakes were low, they were never allowed to make their own decisions but were trained to listen to a voice outside of their heads—that of their parents. However, when they reach their teen years and no longer want to listen to their parents, they still follow that same pattern, only this time the voice outside of their heads no longer belongs to their parents; it belongs to their "friends." Drill sergeant parents tend to create kids who are followers because they have never learned how to make decisions for themselves.

Parents send messages to their children about what they think their kids are capable of. The message the helicopter parent sends is, "You are fragile and can't make it without me." The drill sergeant's message is,

"You can't think for yourself, so I'll do it for you." While both of these parental types may successfully control their children in the early years, they will have done their kids a disservice once puberty is reached. Helicopter children become adolescents unable to cope with outside forces, think for themselves, or handle their own problems. Drill sergeant kids, who did a lot of saluting when they were young, will do a lot of saluting when teenagers, but the salute is different: a raised fist or a crude gesture involving the middle finger.

LOVE AND LOGIC TIP 1

The Laissez-Faire Parent

Another lesser parenting type that is worth mentioning here in passing is what we call the laissez-faire parent. These are parents who for one reason or another—whether it is because they are unsure of how to handle their child or have become confused by the variety of parenting opinions and advice out there—decide to let their children raise themselves. Some have bought into the theory that children are innately born with the ability to govern themselves, if just given the time and opportunity, and will eventually grow into successful, creative people if the parent would just stay out of the way and not interfere. Others believe that they should be their child's best friend and that preserving that relationship is more important than teaching the child any form of self-discipline or character. Others feel guilty for working out of the home and spending so little time with their kids. Rather than holding their children accountable for their actions, they simply let them run free, believing that "quality" time will make up for the lack of "quantity" of time they spend with their children and that responsibility will eventually rub off on the children during the right "quality" moments. Still others just don't know what to do anymore, so they have given up trying.

We would like to emphasize that, in fact, this is not really a parenting type but a cop-out or misunderstanding of parenting responsibilities. As Jim likes to say, "If children were meant to run the home, they would have been born larger." While children should be able to decide between safe and responsible options (as we will explain in the next section), we do not advocate letting them decide everything for themselves or even learning from natural consequences that may have damaging effects. The love part of Love and Logic emphasizes the nurturing of the child toward the responsible, competent person the parent and society believe the child can be. This will take some thought and preparation on the parents' part, but as you will see in the following chapters, the results are well worth the effort and involvement.

The Effective Parenting Style of Love and Logic

The Consultant Parent

Helicopters can't hover forever, and eventually drill sergeants go hoarse. Allow us to introduce an alternative, employed by Love and Logic parents, which works well throughout life. While especially effective with teenagers, it also reflects the attitude parents should have from the time their children are toddlers. We call it the consultant parenting style.

As children grow, they move from being concrete thinkers to being abstract thinkers when they are teens. Children need thoughtful guidance and firm, enforceable limits. We set those limits based on the safety of the child and how the child's behavior affects others. Then we must maintain those limits to help children understand that they are responsible for their actions and will suffer reasonable consequences for actions that are inappropriate. However, while the parents are drawing and holding these limits, it is important for them to continue encouraging their children to think about their behavior and help them feel in control of their actions by giving choices within those limits. This is where the consultant parent comes in.

As our children grow into adolescents, this parenting style becomes even more important. Teens often resent guidelines and rebel at firm limits because they've grown to think differently than when they were younger. Because of this important change in cognition, parents must adjust the way they parent to meet the needs of the new thought processes taking place in their adolescents. They step back a bit from being the enforcer of limits and let reasonable, real-world consequences do the teaching. They become advisors and counselors more than police officers, allowing their adolescents to make more decisions for themselves, and then guide them to successfully navigate the consequences of those decisions.[1]

Love and Logic parents avoid the helicopter and drill sergeant mentalities by using a consultant style of parenting as early as possible in the child's life. They ask their children questions and offer choices. Instead of telling their children what to do, they put the burden of decision making on their kids' shoulders. They establish options within limits.[2] Thus, by the time the children become teens, they are used to making good decisions.

The Paradox of Success and Failure

Although we're tempted to do otherwise, we have to admit there is no surefire, absolute, guaranteed-or-your-money-back approach to raising responsible children. No expert in the field can honestly say, "If you operate this way, it'll work every time." Just because we do something correctly doesn't mean it will work out the way we'd hoped.

We all have examples of parents who employ very faulty parenting techniques but whose children come out smelling like roses. And we know of those who do everything "right" but end up raising kids who would make Attila the Hun look like an Eagle Scout.

Nothing in parenting is sure. However, we increase the odds of raising responsible kids when we take thoughtful risks. We do that when we allow our children—get this—*to fail.* In fact, unless we allow them to fail, sometimes grandiosely, we cannot allow our children to choose success.

LOVE AND LOGIC TIP 2

Unfortunately, When Our Gut Talks, Our Head Listens

Love and Logic techniques may rub some parents the wrong way. Allowing kids to fail with love and letting the significant learning opportunities (SLOs) do the teaching are principles that may go against the parental grain. Most of us raise our children based on our gut reactions. But how do we know whether such responses are trustworthy or just the result of bad lasagna?

Actually, adult "gut reactions" are the results of childhood responses to family emotions and interactions. Therefore, "gut feel" is more valid if we had a happy childhood and presently have peaceful and rewarding relationships at home and elsewhere. On the other hand, if we react to our childhood by saying, "I sure want to do things differently with my kid than my mom and dad did with me," then our gut reactions will probably be untrustworthy and faulty.

Don't be alarmed if you feel uneasy with some of the techniques in this book. In fact, if you want to raise your kids in ways different from the way you were raised, your uneasiness probably confirms that you're on the right track in learning the Love and Logic method.

God gave all humans—His supreme creation—considerable freedom, and that includes the opportunity to goof up. Failure and success are two sides of the same coin. If there had been no forbidden tree in the Garden of Eden, humanity would have had no opportunity to make responsible or irresponsible choices. When Adam and Eve made the wrong choice, God allowed them to suffer the consequences. Although He did not approve of their disobedience, He loved them enough to let them make a decision and live with the results.

God's love in the garden sets the example for all parents to follow: He allowed Adam and Eve the freedom to make the choice. In a similar way, if we give children freedom and loving acceptance, they will sometimes make choices and do things we don't approve of.

As our children grow older and gain more power over their lives and environment, the correct exercise of their ability to make decisions becomes even more important for them. Just as God gave us a good mind and the ability to excel, He has given us the capability to blow up the planet. However, a race capable of blowing up the planet is also capable of flying to Saturn. High success and high achievement carry with them the risks of abysmal losses.

On a different scale, the "forbidden fruit" may be drugs, a particular friend, Internet pornography sites, or any number of other things. Smart parents realize that in order for their children to succeed, their kids need to learn to make their own decisions and that, in doing so, sometimes they will exert their independence by choosing, consciously, to fail!

I (Jim) used to insist that my son, Charlie, dress for the weather on chilly Colorado mornings. "Charlie," I'd say, "it's cold out this morning. You'd better wear your heavy coat." Sure enough, he'd grab his little slicker—the lightest coat he owned—and waltz out the door.

Unwittingly, I was taking away his best choice. I thought I was ensuring that Charlie would be warm waiting for the bus, but he chose to be cold instead. He was exerting his free will.

But I wised up. I would instead say, "Charlie, it's twenty degrees out. You might want to wear a coat." This offered him a range of choices from worst to best (kids always seem to discount the first option we give them). In the end, Charlie decided to exert his free will with a warm coat.

So the paradox is that parents who try to ensure their children's successes, often raise unsuccessful kids! But the loving and concerned parents who allow for failure wind up with kids who tend to choose success. These are the parents who take thoughtful risks. As God gives each of us choices, we can do no less for our own beloved children.

The Love and Logic approach helps kids raise their odds of becoming thinking individuals who choose success. As parents, this means we must allow for failures and help our kids make the most of them during their elementary school days, when the price tags are still reasonable.

Learning at Affordable Prices

Today's kids suffer from inflation. The cost of learning how to live in our world is going up daily. The drugs our children will be tempted with are more potent than those we faced even a decade ago, sexually transmitted infections are more widespread and more deadly, the media is more graphic, Internet predators and pornographers are doing more to get to wider audiences, school violence is scarier than ever, and the list goes on. The price a child pays today to learn about friendships, school, learning, commitment, decision making, and responsibility is the cheapest it will ever be. Tomorrow it's always higher.

The older a child gets, the bigger the decisions become and the graver the consequences of those decisions. Little children can make many mistakes at affordable prices. They can pick themselves up and try again if things don't work out. Usually all they're out are some temporary pain and a few tears. This is easy to illustrate.

Giving a three-year-old the choice "Would you like to go to the car with your feet on the ground or in the air?" sets a safe, enforceable limit in response to a rebellious refusal on a rainy night in front of a restaurant. Telling school-aged siblings they can do chores or sell some of their toys to pay for Monica, the babysitter from hell, to come watch them while mom goes to the store is not an unreasonable consequence of their previous tirades on such a shopping trip. Even, to some extent, letting a smart-mouthed boy of five get his face rubbed in the grass a bit because he wised off to bigger, older neighborhood boys will, if he is left to handle his own problem, teach a major-league lesson in respect. Bigger boys rub their hands with glee at the prospect of teaching smart-aleck kids lessons. The lesson for the smaller child may cost a little—a bloody nose or a black eye—but the price is affordable.

Yet these prices are too high for some parents. They protect. They reason, "I love him. I don't want little Johnny to learn the hard way." So they kneel in a puddle on a rainy night and try to plead their toddler into the car. They let their kids run them ragged on trip after trip to the grocery store. Or they yell at the neighborhood boys, "You kids be nice to Johnny. If you can't be nice, I'm going to tell your parents." As a result, the smart-aleck kid loses the opportunity to learn a lesson at blue-light-special prices. Now he may have to learn it at age fifteen, and anyone who has seen fifteen-year-old boys go at it knows that the price tag will be far more expensive.

True, it's painful to watch our kids learn through natural consequences or, as we like to call them, significant learning opportunities (SLOs). But that pain is part of the price we must pay to raise responsible kids. We have a choice though: We can hurt a little as we watch them learn life's lessons now, or we can hurt a lot as we watch them grow up to be individuals unable to care for themselves.

LOVE AND LOGIC TIP 3

You Can Pay Me Now, or You Can Pay Me Later

Shannon had eight kids. Every time I (Jim) visited her house, I saw her handing out money to the kids. One day I asked, "What is this with you dishing out money all the time?"

"We give our kids loans in the household because they're learning about the world of finance," Shannon answered while handing fifty cents to one of her young sons. "Our loans are just like those at First National Bank, with due dates, promissory notes, and collateral. Why, the other day I repossessed a seventy-nine-dollar CD player."

"Must have been sad for the kid," I said.

"Not really," Shannon replied. "That's a gift to him because now my son, who's only twelve years old, knows all about the responsibility of paying back his loans. He knows all about promissory notes and collateral, and even repossession—and it only cost him a seventy-nine-dollar CD player.

"The neighbor kid," Shannon continued, "learned the same lesson when the bank came and repossessed his $4,900 Camaro. He's twenty-six, but his parents protected him when he was young. My son has a fourteen-year head start on the guy."

To Protect Them Is Not to Love Them

America needs kids who can handle tough times, especially in this post-9/11, post-Hurricane Katrina world. Many issues Americans must face in our schools and cities occur as acts of nature or terrorism. However, our homes give many coping opportunities of their own. Generally, children take their cue on how to deal with such challenges from the adults in the environment they share. Learning how to handle small things—and especially to fail at small things and grow through that affordable experience—is the best way to prepare our children for whatever they may face in the future.

Too many parents confuse *love*, *protection*, and *caring*. These concepts are not synonymous. Parents may refuse to allow their children to fail because they see such a response as uncaring. Thus, they overcompensate with worry and hyper-concern.

What these parents are doing, in reality, is meeting their own selfish needs. They make more work for themselves and will, in the long run, raise children who make their own lives more work. *Protection* is not synonymous with *caring*, but both are a part of love.

Let's look at the way God operates. If we ask ourselves, "Does God care about us?" we'd probably respond, "Sure, God cares a lot about us." But if we then ask ourselves, "Would He let us jump off a cliff tonight?" we'd all have to admit, "Yeah, now that you mention it, He probably would." So does He *care*? Of course He does! Yet God loves without being overly protective.

Caring for our children does not equate to protecting them from every possible misstep they could make in growing up. Of course, when their child is an infant, responsible parents must respond to him with total protectiveness. Every problem the infant encounters really is the parents' problem. If parents do not protect the infant, he will die.

However, as children grow—beginning at about nine months of age with very simple choices—the parents must make a gentle, gradual transition to allowing their children the privilege of solving their own problems. By the time children are eleven or twelve years old, they should be able to make most decisions without parental input. Actually, to be truthful, parental love and attitude determine how children will handle most problems through early adolescence.

For instance, think about a group of mothers watching their toddlers wobble onto the ice during their first time on skates. Once the toddlers make their first inevitable crash on the ice, one group of moms, worried to death at the side of the rink, yells, "Are you hurt?" And the toddlers, scrunching up their face and sliding back toward Mom, say, in that distinctive toddler way, "Yeah, come to think of it, I *am* hurt." The other group of moms merely shouts, "Kaboom!" when the children go down, and their youngsters pick themselves up, dust a few flakes off the old bottom, and go on skating, often saying, "Yeah, kaboom!" in agreement.

The first group of children learned that a fall is a painful experience. The second group learned from their mistakes, not concentrating on the pain and parental rescue. The problem is, rescuing parents often rescue out of their own needs. They like to heal hurts. They are parents who need to be needed, not parents who want to be wanted.

Children who have been shown love primarily by protection may be irreparably damaged by the time they reach high school. Parents of middle or high school children who must concern themselves with clothing, television habits, homework, teeth brushing, haircuts, and the like have "at-risk" children on their hands. At the very least, these children are not going to be much fun for their future spouse.

The challenge of parenting is to love kids enough to allow them to fail—to stand back, however painful it may be, and let SLOs build our children.

Responsibility Cannot Be Taught

Parents are forever moaning about their children's inability to absorb parental words of wisdom. It seems we can tell daughter Kayla a hundred times not to forget something, and sure enough, she walks out the door without it. We tell son Ryan to show some respect, and he answers, "Why do I have to do that? You're living in the Dark Ages!"

One thing for sure we can't tell kids is "Be responsible." It doesn't work. Have you ever noticed that the parents who yell the loudest about responsibility seem to have the most irresponsible kids? The most responsible children usually come from families in which parents almost never use the word *responsibility.* It's a fact: Responsibility cannot be taught; it must be caught.

To help our children gain responsibility, we must offer them opportunities to be responsible. That's the key. Parents who raise responsible kids spend very little time and energy worrying about their kids' responsibilities; they worry more about how to let the children encounter SLOs for their *irresponsibility.* They are involved with their kids, certainly, lovingly using good judgment as to when their children are ready to learn the next level of life's lessons. But they don't spend their time reminding them or worrying for them. In a subtle way, they're saying, "I'm sure you'll remember on your own, but if you don't, you'll surely learn something from the experience." These parents help their children understand they can solve their own problems. These parents are sympathetic but don't solve their kids' problems.

Children who grow in responsibility also grow in self-esteem, a prerequisite for achievement in the real world. As their self-esteem and self-confidence grow, children are better able to make it once the parental ties are cut.

3

Responsible Children Feel Good About Themselves

Even children make themselves known by their acts, by whether what they do is pure and right.
Proverbs 20:11

There are two types of kids in this world. One type gets up in the morning, looks in the mirror, and says, "Hey, look at that dude. He's all right! I like that guy, and I bet other people will like him too." The other type, when he looks in the mirror, says, "Oh, no, look at that boy. I really don't like what I see, and I bet other people won't like him either."

Two radically different outlooks on life; two radically different self-concepts. Children with a poor self-concept often forget to do homework, bully other kids, argue with teachers and parents, steal, and withdraw into themselves whenever things get rocky—irresponsible in all they do. Children with a good self-concept tend to have a lot of friends, do their chores regularly, and don't get into trouble in school—they take responsibility as a matter of course in their daily lives. Although this may seem simplistic, there is a direct correlation between self-concept and performance in school, at home, on the playground, or wherever children may be. Kids learn best and are responsible when they feel good about themselves.

When parenting with Love and Logic, we strive to offer our children a chance to develop that needed positive self-concept. With love enough to allow the children to fail, with love enough to allow the consequences of their actions to teach them about responsibility, and with love enough to help them celebrate the triumphs, our children's self-concept will grow each time they survive on their own.

I Am What I Think You Think I Am

Unfortunately, many parents don't give their children a chance to build a positive self-concept; instead, they concentrate on their children's weaknesses. They reason (often unknowingly), "Before my Elizabeth can be motivated to learn anything, she has to know how weak she is." Whenever these parents talk to their children, the conversation centers on what the children are doing poorly or what they can't do. If a child has trouble with fractions or has sloppy work habits or doesn't pronounce syllables properly—whatever the problem—the parents let him or her know about these weaknesses continually. The result is a constant eroding of their child's self-concept. But parents who build on their kids' strengths find their children growing in responsibility almost daily.

Think of how we, as adults, respond to a person who builds on our strengths. If somebody very important to us thinks we're the greatest thing since remote controls, we will perform like gangbusters for that person. But if that important person thinks we're the scum of the earth, we will probably never prove him or wrong.

It's the same way with kids. Kids say to themselves, *I don't become what* you think *I can, and I don't become what* I think *I can. I become what* I think you think *I can.* Then they spend most of their emotional energy looking for proof that what they think is our perception of them is correct. For example, long before Jim's son, Charlie, developed his writing skills, his seventh-grade teacher raved about his writing potential, building him up and encouraging him. Responding to what his teacher thought he could do, Charlie worked on his writing with determination and enthusiasm and is now an accomplished psychologist, public speaker, and author of several books.

As parents, we play an integral part in the building of a positive self-concept in our children. In our words and through our actions, in how we encourage and how we model, the messages we give our kids shape the way they feel about themselves. Unfortunately, many of the really powerful messages we send our children have covert negative meanings. We may mean well, but sometimes the words we use and the way we phrase them are received by our children as something totally different from what we meant to say. This is one of the severe tragedies of parent-child relationships.

For example, a simple question such as, "What are you doing that for?" packs a double meaning. The overt message seems like a simple question. However, what our child hears underneath is, "You're not very competent." When we say, "If I've told you once, I've told you a thousand times," the implication is, "You're pretty dumb, and your neurons work sluggishly."

Such implied messages are put-downs, the kind of messages that would make us fighting mad if they were said to us by a supervisor or a coworker. We can lace these messages with as much syrup as the human voice is capable of carrying—"Now, honey, you're not going without your coat today, are you?"—but the implied message still shines through; namely, "You're not smart enough to know whether or not your own body is hot or cold." The ultimate implied message says, "I'm bigger than you are. I'm more powerful than you are. I have more authority, and I can make you do things."

Whenever we order our children to "Shut up!" "Stop arguing!" or "Turn off the television!" we're sending a message that slashes into their self-concept. Why is this? Because, when we give children orders, we are saying:

- "You don't take suggestions."
- "You can't figure out the answer for yourself."
- "You have to be told what to do by a voice outside your head."

Conversely, when we parent with Love and Logic, we emphasize a powerful combination: letting our children fail in nonthreatening situations while emphasizing their strengths. We must be uncritical and unprotective. Parents who raise irresponsible children do exactly the opposite! They're critical *and* protective.

LOVE AND LOGIC TIP 4

What We Say Is Not Always What Kids Hear

Kids are quick to understand the underlying messages we give, whether they come through our words or our actions. Each of the following examples carries both an overt and a covert meaning.

"Isabella, I'll let you decide that for yourself."
OVERT MESSAGE: "You can decide."
COVERT MESSAGE: "You are capable."

"Trevor, I'll give you one more chance, but you better shape up."
OVERT MESSAGE: "Things better improve."
COVERT MESSAGE: "You can't handle it. I have to provide another chance."

"Why in the world did you do that, Michael?"
OVERT MESSAGE: A simple question.
COVERT MESSAGE: "That was very foolish."

"Don't go out without your coat, Tessa."
OVERT MESSAGE: A simple reminder.
COVERT MESSAGE: "You're not capable of thinking for yourself."

The Three-Legged Table of Self-Concept

The building of a person's self-concept can be compared to building a three-legged table. Such a table will stand only when all three supports are strong. If any one of the legs is weak, the table will wobble and rock. If a leg is missing, goodbye table.

Our children's three-legged table of self-concept is built through the implied messages we give. These messages either build them up and allow them to succeed by themselves or add to childhood discouragement and reduced self-esteem.

LOVE AND LOGIC TIP 5

A Tale of Self-Concept

The first day of kindergarten. Big school. Big bus. Big moment in a child's life. Elena and Brady—two very different kinds of kids—walk through the school doors on that very big first day. In Elena's head, the thinking goes,

School's probably going to be fun. I'll get a fair shot. I can learn. School is really no big deal. In Brady's head, the music is not so harmonious: *School may not be that great. I may not be able to learn. I may have a hard time with friends. I really don't know about this school business.*

A child's self-concept is deeply entrenched by the time that child hits kindergarten, built through the many implied messages he or she received during the first few years of life. From the moment of birth, a child embarks on a lifelong mission of feeling accepted and being noticed in a positive way.

Elena picked up all kinds of positive messages during her first five years—messages that she was capable, lovable, and valuable. Her parents sent signals that said, "We love you the way you are because you are you." At a very early age, Elena was given opportunities to do her own thinking. The decisions were about elementary issues, true, but they were decisions nonetheless. Her parents asked such things as, "Do you want to wear your coat today, or do you want to carry it?"

Brady picked up messages, too, but those messages told him he was not measuring up to parental expectations. The messages he heard said, "We could have a lot more love for you if you would just do better." Brady was never allowed to decide anything. When it came time to put on his coat, his parents said, "You get that coat on. You're not going out without it."

On that first day of school, Elena had very few doubts about her ability, but Brady was filled with questions, misgivings, and a lack of confidence. When the first assignment sheet was passed out, Elena jumped right on it and gave it her best shot. But Brady held back. He stalled. He needed encouragement. A voice inside his head said, "You may not do as well as the others. Watch out! You're going to be hurt." Brady didn't want to look bad, so he avoided completing—or even starting—his work.

By sixth grade, Elena will probably have continued in success, every small victory building on an already healthy self-concept. But Brady will probably be apathetic, avoiding all challenges and making life miserable for his parents and teachers.

Building a child's self-concept begins at home, and it begins from the moment of birth.

Leg One: I Am Loved by the "Magical People" in My Life

The best kind of love is the love that comes with no strings attached. Our love for our children must never be conditional. This is not easy, but the benefits are enormous. Genuine love must be shown regardless of the kids' accomplishments. That does not mean, however, that we approve of all their actions.

All too often, parents don't give their kids the chance to experience their love. Some withhold love as a way of making children behave better or break bad habits. Others, in their zeal to help youngsters improve schoolwork, for example, exert so much "love" getting them to do their homework that the children receive covert messages that real love will have to wait until they improve. These parents express their love through intensity and pressure, forgetting the real signs of love (eye contact, smiles, and so on); and the kids, very tuned in to nonverbal communication, see this and think their parents' love depends on their achievement in school. In reality, the interaction between parents and children—the expression of love—is far more important than the kids' successes or failures. Here's another paradox: Kids can't get better until we prove to them, beyond a shadow of a doubt, that they're good enough the way they are.

Strong, effective parents say in both their covert and overt messages, "There's a lot of love here for you regardless of the way you act or do your work at school or anyplace else." When this love is combined with pats on the back, hugs, a smile, and eye contact, a tight bond is created between parent and child. Children never get too old for this experience. (How do you feel when someone treats you this way?) Such a combination packs powerful messages. Kids remember these messages for a lifetime when they come from the "magical people" in their lives—close family members and special teachers. They subconsciously—even consciously—set out to prove that their magical people are correct.

Leg Two: I Have the Skills I Need to Make It

To build children's self-concept, parents must send messages that tell their children they have the skills people their age need to be successful. Each child must feel he or she can compete with other kids in the classroom, on the ball field, at home—anywhere kids interact. Children must know that within themselves are the necessary ingredients to handle life and that they have the abilities to succeed.

These skills are learned through modeling. Good parental models help children develop good attitudes and feelings about themselves. To be good models, parents must realize that children are always watching them and taking cues on how to act and react. Wise parents think, *Don't get too uptight if our children don't always listen to us, but tremble in fear that they see what we do.*

LOVE AND LOGIC TIP 6

Messages That Lock In Love

A lot of bonding goes on between parents and children, especially dads and boys when there is friendly wrestling, arm wrestling, shoving, and playful punching. This physical contact between fathers and sons can lock in messages such as, "We enjoy goofing around together," "You're tough," "You're growing up," and "You're just too strong for me anymore."

Kids are born with a great capacity to learn to do things the way big people do. They observe and attempt to copy what they see. Their prime interest is learning and doing things just like their parents do them. All too often, however, parents discourage their kids with the model they present.

Tyler sees his dad sweeping the garage. He grabs a little broom and starts moving dirt around, imitating his father. Inside, Tyler is thinking, *I feel big. I am learning how to use the broom. I hope Dad notices.*

Dad notices all right. He notices all the spots the little tyke is missing, rather than appreciating the learning that is taking place. "Tyler!" he says, his voice dripping with disapproval. "Look at the mess you're making! Please go play and let me finish this."

If Dad pulls this once in a while (we all do), Tyler's self-concept will come out of it unscathed, but habitual discouragement will lead to a poor self-concept in the child. He'll stop trying to imitate responsible "adult" behavior because he sees himself as incapable.

Parents who routinely focus on the end result rather than on the learning taking place wind up with kids who have a negative self-concept about their skills. Then parents wonder why their kids never want to help around the house.

"But what about quality control?" you may be asking. "When do we start worrying about the end results? We don't want unswept dust piles in the garage forever, do we?" The quality of learning improves with practice, encouragement, and modeling. Say, "Gee, Tyler, you really know how to sweep. Isn't it fun to do a good job? Watch how I use the broom and get *all* of the dirt." This gives the child a good model to copy. Like Dad, Tyler wants to do a good job and feel good about it too.

When children are small, we can teach them a great combination: *getting the job done*, *fun*, and *me*. We make sure that getting the job done is fun. We model that. We never pass judgment on the work of children when they are trying to learn. Rather, we say such things as:

- "I can see that you are working hard to learn to do long division. Let me know if you would like some help."
- "I see that you are learning to make the bed just like Mommy. Would you like me to show you how I get the wrinkles out?"

Whenever possible, we slip a little fun in the task. When Foster's children were small and he did the dishes with them, he encouraged them to imagine the unhappiness of the germs on the dishes as they rinsed them off before putting them into the dishwasher. "What's going on here?" the germs would scream. "What's that big rag doing? It's wiping me off the plate. Arrrrgghh!" Then, as the germs went down the garbage disposal, they continued their dialogue: "What's this big round room? What's going on in here? Hey, guys, it's starting to spin. We're all going to get killed! Arrrgghh!" When his children were high school age, they were still imagining the germs screaming and dying.

It would have been easy to come down on them when they were little for missing a spot here and there, but that would have spoiled the fun. As our children grow up, we remove ourselves from the triad, and they are left with the job and fun. Then we are elsewhere, having fun doing our own jobs.

Leg Three: I Am Capable of Taking Control of My Life

Children with a strong third leg on the three-legged table listen to a little voice in their head that says, "I am capable of taking control of my life. I can make decisions, and I am strong enough to live with the good and the bad consequences of my decisions." Children who say this have been allowed to make decisions about the things that affect them directly.

Many parents tell their children they expect them to be responsible for themselves, yet these same parents are forever informing their kids when they are hot, cold, hungry, thirsty, or tired, or even when they need to go to the bathroom. We've all heard these messages:

- "Put on your coat. It's too cold for you to be going out without it."
- "You can't be hungry. We just ate an hour ago."
- "Sit down and be quiet. You don't need another drink."
- "You get to sleep right this minute!"
- "Be sure to use the bathroom before we leave."

Each of these messages tells children they are not capable of thinking for themselves, that they cannot take control of their life and make decisions. Interestingly, such messages often come from parents who moan and groan about their kids' lack of responsibility and ability to think for themselves.

LOVE AND LOGIC TIP 7

It Can Be a Cold World Out There

It was a frigid Colorado evening, and my (Foster's) family was heading out on an errand. Gathered at the door, my wife asked our six-year-old son, "Andrew, do you want to wear your coat?"

He said, "No, I don't need my coat." He was wearing a T-shirt. Modeling responsible adult behavior, my wife said, "I'm sure glad I'm wearing my coat." Then she put on her coat, and the family got into the car.

Two blocks from home, muffled sounds came drifting from the backseat—the unmistakable sounds of shivering and teeth chattering. My wife said, "Do I detect goose bumps in the backseat?"

"Y-y-eah-h-h!" Andrew stuttered. The next words spoken were some of the wisest ever to pass from Andrew's lips: "N-n-n-ext time, I'm g-g-g-oing to wear my c-c-c-oat!"

"Oh, honey, that sounds like a good idea." (Our drive lasted long enough for the message to sink in, but not so long that Andrew turned blue.)

Had my wife said, "Wear your coat. It's cold out," Andrew probably would have said, "No." And she would have said, "I'm your mother, wear your coat." Then Andrew would have been sitting in the backseat, warm as toast, hating her, and not learning a thing. He would have been thinking, *Okay, I'll wear my coat, but only because you made me. Just wait until I'm old enough to decide for myself about wearing a coat!*

When little kids rebel, parents can quash the rebellion with a stern order and get good short-term results. But when kids hit adolescence and rebel, parental orders too often become unenforceable. Allowing children at a young age to practice decision making on simple issues teaches them to think and control their own lives. Then when adolescence hits, they will be less susceptible to peer pressure regarding alcohol, drugs, sex, and other temptations. They will have learned they can make their own wise decisions. Those kids can become their parents' very best friends during the tough teenage years. They can also become their own best friend.

Although kids are born with great courage to take control of their own lives and make decisions, they have little experience on which to base their decisions, so they often make poor choices. But they can learn from those mistakes, provided parents don't get too involved.

The Difference Between Praise and Encouragement

Every parent wants their child to develop a positive self-image, and every parent knows that a positive self-image is related to feeling good about accomplishments. Understandably, parents concentrate on evaluating a child's job and want their child to feel good about what he or she has done. The easiest and perhaps most natural thing is to praise the child in the belief or hope that the child will accept praise and feel great about himself.

Some parents view praise as so important that even when their child does a bad job, they still make the assumption that praise is called for. For example, we saw a father in a park watching his son fly a model airplane, and although the plane would crash with great frequency after increasingly short flights, the father would exclaim with feigned joy, "What a great flight!" We watched his child's expression, and there was no doubt he wondered,

- *Is Dad blind?*
- *Is Dad lying?*
- *Doesn't poor Dad know what a good flight is?*
- *Does Dad think I'm blind?*
- *Does Dad think I need his response?*

In the end, false praise almost always leads to disrespect.

Love and Logic teaches that effective praise is built on two assumptions:

1. The evaluator and those evaluated have a good relationship or at least mutual respect.
2. The evaluator is in a position to judge the "goodness" of the action or production.

When either of these assumptions is not true, praise falls flat. Encouragement has several advantages over praise:

- It makes no assumptions about the relationship. It can be bad, neutral, or good.
- It assumes children can judge their own behavior or output and make decisions on how to (or not to) modify things in the future.
- It always accepts the evaluation of the child, even if the self-evaluation is too harsh.

If the self-evaluation is too harsh, praisers often end up arguing with the child. For instance:

ADULT: "What a beautiful painting!"
CHILD: "I don't think so."
ADULT: "Why not?"
CHILD: "The nose is too big." (Now the judgment of the evaluator is being questioned, so the argument begins.)
ADULT: "I'm not so sure that's true."
CHILD: "Well, it is."
ADULT: "I don't think so!"
CHILD: "Is too!"
ADULT: "Is not."
The situation is different with encouragement:
ADULT: (with a happy and encouraging voice) "Wow, what do you think of your picture?"
CHILD: "I don't like it."

ADULT: "Why is that?"
CHILD: "The nose is too big."
ADULT: "Really! How'd that happen?"
CHILD: "I have trouble with noses."
ADULT: "So how will all this turn out?"
CHILD: "Great, 'cause I'm practicing 'em, and I'm getting better."

When children have a poor self-image, praise almost always causes the child to act out. Because the praising comment does not fit with the child's self-image, the child then acts worse to instruct the adult about the real situation. If a child is very negative, it might be wise for the evaluator to say, "Gee, if I did a job like that, I would probably feel better about myself than you seem to, but everyone is different."

The chart on the following page clarifies the differences between praise and encouragement. Note how encouragement helps children feel great about their achievement because they self-evaluate and think for themselves. Praise isn't bad, but notice how its emphasis is on external evaluation—the joy of another—and no real thinking is encouraged.

Positive Self-Esteem Comes from Accomplishment

Kids get the most out of what they accomplish for themselves. Children will get more out of making their own decision—even if it is wrong—than they will out of parents making that decision for them. Sometimes that means standing by as our kids struggle to complete a task we could easily help them with or do for them.

It is normal for parents to want their children to have nice things and not have to struggle as much as the parents did growing up. However, that does not mean that because parents have the money (or, unfortunately, the credit limit) to buy their children whatever they want, they should buy it for them, nor does it mean that if they have the clout to get their kids out of a tough spot, they should do so. If we never let our kids struggle to get something they want or work through a problem for themselves, then when things get difficult later in life, they won't suddenly turn tough and get going; instead, they'll just quit. Ultimately, believing in themselves as capable human beings comes

	Praise	Encouragement
Location	Good feelings from the outside	Builds good feelings from the inside
Technique	Statements	Questions
Assumes	Child and adult have good relationship	No assumptions about relationship
Content	Judgmental	Nonjudgmental
Results when child has a good self-image and likes the adult	Feels good about job and adult	Feels more competent in making decisions Feels good about self
Results when child's self-image is poor	Discounts with: "He's just trying to make me feel better. He doesn't really know me." Acts out negative behavior to prove how bad he really is	Feelings toward adult unchanged May be better able to self-evaluate In no case does behavior worsen if asked nonjudgmental questions
Examples	"What a great job!" "You did so well!" "I bet you feel proud of yourself!"	"How do you think you did?" "Why is that?" "How did you figure that out?" "How do you think you will handle it next time?"

from accomplishing difficult things, not having those things done for them or being repeatedly told they are great kids.

Beyond our encouraging words, the pattern for building self-esteem and self-confidence looks something like this in almost every case:

1. Kids take a risk and try to do something they think they can't.
2. They struggle in the process of trying to do it.
3. After a time, they accomplish what they first set out to do.
4. They get the opportunity to reflect back on their accomplishment and can say, "Look at what I did!"

The final steps of forming a positive self-concept as our kids grow is an inside job—it is something kids have to do for themselves. It comes from working hard and accomplishing good things. No amount of stuff or praise can build a resilient self-image for children. Oddly enough, kids don't feel good about themselves when we do everything we can to keep them happy or give them everything they want. They have to sweat a little and earn things for themselves.

Of course, if we let them risk accomplishing difficult things, it means they might just as easily fail as succeed. They must know we love them whether they succeed or not, and we can support and encourage them along the way as long as we don't take their efforts away from them. By letting our kids work their way through age-appropriate tough times when they are younger, we are preparing them to effectively face truly tough times down the road.

Again, this must be used with common sense. We don't need to artificially create difficult situations for them, nor do we let them struggle with things too far beyond their abilities. For a toddler, building a block tower can be equivalent to a twelve-year-old learning to play a moderately difficult piece of music on the piano, but if we reversed these roles, the situations would be ridiculous. Love and Logic parents prepare for such situations and know how to keep the work and decision making in their kid's court rather than in their own.

If We're Happy, They're Happy

You may find this an extremely distressing thought, but kids learn nearly every interpersonal activity by modeling. And you know who their primary models are, don't you? The way they handle fighting, frustration, solving problems, getting along with other people, language, posture, movements—everything is learned by watching the big people in their lives. Their all-seeing eyes are scoping out our actions, from learning to talk to learning to drive.

By the time children are toilet trained, they're dressing up in Mom's shoes or wearing Dad's hat. If Mom's at the sink doing dishes, there they are too, splashing around and getting totally soaked. If Dad's under the hood tinkering with the carburetor, there the kids are, lending their own "helping" hand. Many parents get irritated and feel it's a bother having the kids underfoot. But what learning opportunities—at low price tags!

LOVE AND LOGIC TIP 8

What They See Is What They Learn

I (Jim) spent my childhood on the wrong side of the tracks in a trailer in industrial Denver. When my family scraped enough money together, we bought a little garage to live in while my dad built a house on the property.

Dad worked a morning shift downtown and rode the streetcar to work, and then when he returned at 2:00 p.m. every day, he picked up his hammer and saw and built a house. It took seven years. As I watched him work, I thought, *Wow! He gets to do all the fun stuff: mix the concrete, lay the bricks, put on the shingles, hammer nails, saw wood.* I watched it all day, every day.

At the end of the day, when my dad knocked off, he invariably said, "Jim, clean up this mess." So I would roll out the wheelbarrow, pick up a shovel and a rake, and clean up the mess. At the same time, Dad would explain to me that people have to learn to clean up after themselves. They need to finish and put the tools away.

When my dad noticed that I left my own stuff lying around, he complained, "Why don't you ever pick up your stuff, Jim? There's your bike on the sidewalk, and your tools are all over the place. When you go to look for a tool, you won't know where it is." I, of course, was learning all about cleaning up. I was learning that adults *don't* clean up after themselves.

Had my father modeled cleaning up after himself—saying in the process, "I feel good now that the day's work is finished, but I'll feel better when I clean up this mess and put all the tools in the right places"—he would have developed a son who liked to clean up his own messes. As it is, my garage is a mess to this very day.

The key to parental modeling may sound strange to you, but it goes like this: I always model responsible, healthy adult behavior by taking good care of myself. The maxim of taking good care of ourselves—even putting ourselves first—may go against our parental grain. Many parents believe that their kids should always come first. No sacrifice is too great. These parents are taxi driver, delivery service, alarm clock, travel agent, and financial analyst—all at the same time. However, children growing up with this arrangement see that their parents are not taking care of themselves in a healthy way. They're always putting the children first and themselves last. The kids will then model this behavior by putting themselves last as well.

When high school rolls around, these same parents will wonder why their children have such a poor self-image. After all, the parents say, "I always put them first. I always did everything for them." In reality, young people with a poor self-image are following their parental model. In the same self-depriving way, they're putting themselves last.

Of course, as parents we never put ourselves first at the expense of our children. We don't want them to lose out. We want them to win, but we should want to win as well. Thus, we always strive for a win-win situation. We want to feel good, and we want our children to feel good, so we model taking care of ourselves in a nice, healthy way.

We still take our children places. We do things for them. But healthy people generally desire for things to be a two-way street—a situation where *both* parties win. So we enjoy taking our daughter to her soccer game not only because she enjoys it but also because we enjoy being with her and giving her the chance to excel. We like taking our son to his music lesson because we feel great watching his progress, chatting with him in the car, and generally enhancing the life that he happily reflects back to us.

For many unhappy parents and their entitled, demanding children, life becomes a one-way street. The parent does things for the child, but the child feels no need to repay the parent or make the trips pleasant for the adult. The child only takes, and the parent only gives. Wise parents who find themselves in such a predicament set the model by taking good care of themselves. A Love and Logic parent might say, "Honey, I know you want me to (help you with your homework; take you to your practice; drive you to the movie). However, I'm sorry to say that taking you places (doing things for you) has put a darkening cloud over my haze of happiness lately. That's sad but true. So I think I'll pass on doing it this time." This parent will raise respectful, thoughtful children who grow to take good care of themselves too.

4

Children's Mistakes Are Their Opportunities

How much better to get wisdom than gold!
To get understanding is
to be chosen rather than silver.
Proverbs 16:16

Doug and Sara had a big problem with ten-year-old Austin. Everything they told Austin to do, he did. Whether it was chores, studying hard, getting along with others, or showing respect for adults and teachers, Austin came through flawlessly. Austin got up on his own every day. He always stacked his school stuff neatly by the door before strolling to breakfast, and he always gave himself enough time to enjoy his meal at a leisurely pace. He never walked out without his lunch, assignments, gym clothes, permission slips, or anything else. He consistently reached the bus stop five minutes early. He rarely got into trouble at school. His teachers liked him; he had lots of friends. When he hopped off the bus in the afternoon, he jumped right into his chores and his homework without being told. At the first evening yawn, he decided to turn in for the night—often a good half hour before required. One Saturday morning, the kid cleaned out the garage before Doug and Sara even got out of bed!

Some parents would kill for such "problems" with their kids. But Doug and Sara sat up at night worrying about Austin. "He might go through his childhood years with very few opportunities to grow from his mistakes," they reasoned.

Most of us don't "suffer" from Doug and Sara's problem. Our kids mess up plenty. As they do, they will have more than enough chances to grow in responsibility as they resolve their problems.

LOVE AND LOGIC TIP 9

Responsible Kids, Irresponsible Kids

The most responsible kids I (Jim) encountered during my three decades in the education field were the kids at an inner-city school where I served as an assistant principal. They all hailed from federally funded housing projects. Those kids woke up in the morning without an alarm clock and got to school in time for breakfast without any assistance from their parents. They knew that if they got there, they got breakfast; if they didn't, they missed it. They never missed a bus when it was going someplace they wanted to go.

The most irresponsible kids I ever saw were in an upper-middle-class suburban school. The first day of school, a thousand kids arrived in eighteen different buses. Half of these kids ran straight to the playground for some pre-bell frolic; the other half raced directly to the principal's office to phone their folks for forgotten registration materials, coats, and lunches.

Responsible behavior has a direct correlation to the number of decisions children are expected to make. The more they make, the more responsible they become.

Mother, Please, I'd Rather Do It Myself

Oftentimes we impede our kids' growth. We put ourselves exactly where we shouldn't be: in the middle of their problems. Parents who take on their kids' problems do them a great disservice. They rob their children of the chance to grow in responsibility, and they actually foster further irresponsible behavior.

The greatest gift we can give our children is the knowledge that with God's help, they can always look first to themselves for the answers to their problems. Kids who develop an attitude that says, *I can probably find my own solutions*, become survivors. They have an edge in learning, relating to others, and making their way in the world. That's because the best solution to any problem lies within the skin of the person who owns the problem.

When we solve problems for our kids — the ones they could handle on their own — they're never quite satisfied. Our solution is never quite good enough. When we tell our kids what to do, deep down they say, *I can think for myself*, so oftentimes they do the exact opposite of what we want them to do.

Our anger doesn't help either. Certainly, it galls us to no end when our kids mess up something in their own lives. When they lose schoolbooks or bring home failing grades, it's only natural for us to explode in a living, breathing Fourth-of-July display. But anytime we explode at children for something they do to themselves, we only make the problem worse. We give kids the message that the actual, logical consequence of messing up is making adults mad. The children get swept away in the power of their anger rather than learn a lesson from the consequences of their mistake.

When we intrude into our children's problems with anger or a rescue mission, we make their problems our problems. And children don't worry about problems they know are the concern of their parents. This can be explained partly by the "No sense in both of us worrying about it" syndrome.

Before Jim met his wife, Shirley, he harbored a great dislike for going to the gas station, simply because he hated to part with the money. The only thing that forced him to visit the pumps was a near-empty reading on the fuel gauge. However, when he married Shirley, she discovered this habit and, fearful that he would run out of gas, took on the responsibility of either reminding him to fill the tank or filling it herself. He never had to worry about it; she had his problem well in hand.

After a while, though, Shirley got tired of this irresponsibility and stopped rescuing Jim. One night, he ran out of gas, walked down a dark road for help, stepped off a bridge, and tumbled ten feet into a streambed. Jim was laid up for eight weeks before he walked again. It was then that he realized Shirley was willing to worry about how much gas was in her car but unwilling to worry about the gas in his. Guess who has never run out of gas since? If Shirley wasn't going to worry about that, somebody had better.

Kids who deal directly with their own problems are moved to solve them. They know that if they don't, nobody will. Not their parents, not their teachers—nobody. And on a subconscious level, they feel much better about themselves when they handle their own problems.

You Have Your Troubles, I Have Mine

The list of kids' problems is endless: getting to school on time, getting to school at all, being hassled by friends, hassling friends, harassing teachers, being harassed by teachers, poor grades, laziness, wrong choice of friends, drugs, alcohol, and many, many more. Parents who involve themselves in all of these problems can spend their every waking hour at the task. Unfortunately, these parents believe they show their love for their children by jumping into these conflicts and rescuing them.

LOVE AND LOGIC TIP 10

When to Step In/When to Stay Out of Kids' Problems

Occasionally, we should make our children's problems our problems:

- We step in when our children are in definite danger of losing life or limb or of making a decision that could affect them for a lifetime.
- We step in when our children know they are in a situation they can't handle by themselves. More important, perhaps, is that they know *we* also know they can't handle it. So when we step in and help them out—saying in essence, "You are incapable of coping with this situation"—it is not a destructive message because everyone is aware of the child's inability to handle the situation.

For instance, in a rare circumstance, parents might insist that their child change classrooms. This should happen only if the child is suffering so greatly that his or her entire school future could be threatened and when the child knows that he or she is in an inevitable losing situation. As soon as the parent steps in, the child gets the "You can't cope" message.

Remember: Everything we fix for our kids, our kids will be unable to fix for themselves. If Anna has trouble on the school bus and we haul on down to the stop one morning to talk to the driver and the other kids, Anna is robbed of any chance of handling that problem by herself and will believe that she can't.

If there's more than a 20 percent chance our child might be able to work it out, we should keep clear of owning the problem and not rob our child of the opportunity to learn and grow from the experience.

Even when a kid doesn't seem concerned about his or her problems, we should stay out of them. A child's laziness, for example, is still a child's problem. While untouched homework, bad grades, or tardiness at school may be maddening to us, we must find a loving way to allow the consequences to do the teaching for the child, whatever those consequences might be.[3]

On the other hand, some of the children's behaviors *are* our problems. If the problem is how our children relate to us (disrespectful talk, sassing, rude gestures or behavior), how they do chores, playing loud music, waking us up in the middle of the night, misbehaving when in public, or matters surrounding their life support system (bread and butter, room and board), then the problem has drifted out of their domain and directly into ours. In short, if it's a problem for us, it should soon be a problem for them.

If Connor shoots off his mouth at school, we let the teachers take care of the consequences with our support. But if Connor shoots his mouth off at us, we deal with it.

If Mariah's slowness in getting ready for school makes her late, we stay clear of the problem. But if Mariah's slowness in getting ready to leave the house makes *us* late, we deal with it.

If Caden's room is a nationally declared disaster area, we let him wallow in the mire. But if Caden trashes the living room within fifteen seconds of arrival, that affects us, so we help him handle it—our way.

Again, we are modeling appropriate adult behavior. We don't allow other people to harm us, and we therefore raise children who know how to care for themselves and won't allow others to cause them problems.

LOVE AND LOGIC TIP 11

The "Uh-Oh" Song

Four-year-old Jasmine comes into the kitchen and wants a snack. Because there's only about a half hour left before dinner, her mother tells her that she should wait. Jasmine, however, wants none of this. She continues to beg and plead and finally ends up in a tantrum in the middle of the floor. For many parents this would be the time to hit the roof, but a Love and Logic parent sees the SLO in the situation and is ready for it.

"Uh-oh," Mom says quietly in a sing-songy voice, "looks like someone needs a little private time to pull herself together." Jasmine's head raises and her limbs stop pounding the floor. She has heard this one before and knows what is coming next. Mom scoops Jasmine up lovingly and walks her to her room going through all six steps of using the "Uh-Oh" song:

Step one: Sing out, "Uh-oh! Looks like a little bedroom time," while quickly and gently moving the child to the recovery area. This is often the child's room but can be any other place where the child cannot be with the family.

Step two: Sing, "Feel free to have a nice little fit. We'll see you when you are sweet." Keep your voice melodic while saying this to avoid sounding angry, frustrated, and sarcastic.

Step three: If necessary, offer choices about how the child will stay in the room: "Do you want to stay in your room with the door open or shut?" Then, if the child comes out, you say, "How sad. You chose shut."

If the child comes out again, offer another choice, "Do you want to stay in your room with the door shut or locked? It's your choice." If the child comes out again, you say, "How sad. You chose locked." (Because most doors don't have a lock on the outside, a good solution is to wedge a towel over the top of the door to keep it shut.)

Safety is a prime consideration at this point, so stay close in case of emergency, but do not talk to the child through the door or acknowledge that you are waiting just outside. You can even turn up the TV so that it appears you are having more fun than the child.

Step four: The child will remain in the room until calm. Do not talk to the child during this time even if it sounds like war is going on in the room.

Step five: Once the child is calm, the adult sets the egg timer for four or five minutes. It is important that the child has at least this amount of time to think, *I want to be with the family.*

Step six: Once the child has demonstrated four or five consecutive minutes of calm behavior, he or she returns to the family. The parent should not, and need not, talk with the child about the problem. If there is cleanup necessary because of the misbehavior, the child can do it at this time.

When children misbehave, parents need something they can do to respond, and the more consistent they are in the response, the faster it ingrains itself in the child. That is why we have created the "Uh-Oh" song. It gives parents one catchall response to all attacks on their peace and allows them to respond without anger or threats. Its tone should be devoid of any sarcasm or impatience and almost sung when said to keep any negative emotions out of it. It doesn't take long for even a toddler to get the message that when the "Uh-Oh" song is sung, whatever behavior has just happened was not one Mommy or Daddy approved of and that loving intervention is on its way.

The Two Rules of Love and Logic

Over the years, we have used two principles to guide what we wanted Love and Logic to be: the first was that it had to be as effective as possible, and the second was that we wanted to keep it as simple as possible so that parents could remember it even in the midst of highly emotional times. Because of this, we have summarized the Love and Logic method in two simple rules that will help you do all that we have discussed so far:

Adults must set firm, loving limits using enforceable statements without showing anger, lecturing, or using threats. The statements are enforceable because they deal with how we will respond.

When a child causes a problem, the adult shows empathy through sadness and sorrow and then lovingly hands the problem and its consequences back to the child.

While the rest of this book is dedicated to giving you techniques, tools, and pearls to help follow these two rules in a variety of situations, it is crucial to first understand these two rules as the foundation for all that Love and Logic has to offer you. Because of this, it is worth taking some time here to explore them in more detail before we move on.

Adults must set firm, loving limits using enforceable statements without showing anger, lecturing, or using threats.

Perhaps the most important skill of this first rule is the use of enforceable statements. This is often best done by giving choices that are within your firm, loving limits. For example, if a toddler is acting inappropriately, the parent can sing the "Uh-Oh" song and give him a choice: "Would you like to go to your room walking, or would you like me to carry you?" The limit in this case is that the child cannot act as he just did in the parent's presence and that the best place for the child to be, then, is in his room.

Notice that the parent is not telling the child how to act, such as "Stop that right now!" Such a statement is not enforceable; all it means is that the parent will have to act again if the behavior continues. Nor does the parent simply say, "Go to your room," because that also gives the child the option of disobedience. Instead, two choices are given, both of which are acceptable to the parent and can be enforced if the child decides to do nothing in response. It also shares some modicum of control with the child, and any consequences come from the child's decision, not the parent's.

For example, let's say the child continues to misbehave in response to the question "Would you like to go to your room walking, or would you like me to carry you?" Then the parent can again say, "Uh-oh! It looks as if you chose being carried." Then when the parent deposits the child in the room, the parent can up the ante a bit and show who is really in control of the situation: "Here we are in your room. Feel free to continue your tantrum here if you would like. Would you like to stay in your room with the door open or closed?" If the child decides to flee out the door at that point, then the response is, "Uh-oh! Looks like you chose to be in here with the door shut."

Of course, few kids will probably stop here. A shut door is easily opened again. Then again, when the parent shuts the door, another choice can be given: "Would you like the door just to be shut, or would you like it to be shut and locked? Then I will see you when you are sweet again."

Now, we don't advocate locking children in their rooms and abandoning them there—such actions are tantamount to child abuse. However, if the parent will stay nearby and watchful, she will not have to do this too many times before the child simply chooses to have the door shut and not test it again. If the parent locks the child in the room, she should stay nearby, wait until the tantrum inside has finished, give it a minute or so, and then open the door. We advocate then saying something along the line of, "Oh, I missed you! I am glad to see you are feeling sweeter! Let me set this egg timer to five minutes, and you can come out to be with me again when it goes off if you will stay sweet that whole time."

It is not uncommon after a few interactions like this that the more drastic actions don't have to happen. In fact, many children who grow used to this will hear the "Uh-Oh" song and head toward their rooms without anything else being said.

Of course, the younger the child is when you start using enforceable statements, the easier it is later in life. Here are a few examples:

- "Please feel free to join us for dinner when your room is clean."
- "Would you prefer to wear something nice to church or go in your pajamas?"
- "Feel free to join us in the living room to watch some television once your chores are finished."

- "You are free to use the car as long as your mother or I don't need it, once you have deposited the insurance deductible in a savings account, and as long as I don't have to worry about alcohol or drugs."

While some of these can cause some embarrassing situations (no one really wants to take their kids to church in their pajamas), none of them is dangerous or unenforceable. Certainly, a toddler showing up for church in his pajamas is better than a grade-schooler doing the same, but both are not outlandish.

Make sure that you are willing to enforce whatever choices you give. It won't take too many times of following through on the less desirable choice before your child will understand that either option is truly acceptable to you and that you will carry it out.

By contrast, stay away from alternatives both you and your child know you won't carry out. We would love to have a dollar for every time we have heard a parent at a fast-food restaurant say, "Hurry up and eat, or else I am just going to leave you here!" Both the anger in the comment and the outlandishness of the options just let everyone in earshot know who really was in control of that situation, and the child is more likely to continue racing his fries around his burger than putting anything into his or her mouth.

When a child causes a problem, the adult shows empathy through sadness and sorrow and then lovingly hands the problem and its consequences back to the child.

One of the points of the "Uh-Oh" song is for the parent to show sadness at the actions of their child. Singing the "Uh-Oh" song is simply another way of saying, "Oh, what a sad choice you just made." For older kids, this can change to something along the lines of, "Bummer," or, "Oh, how sad. That never turns out very well for me when I do that," or something else along those lines. The truth of the matter is that consultant parents tend to have very limited vocabularies and respond with the same phrases over and over throughout their children's lives, locking in the fact that parents love them and feel sad when they make the wrong choices. This reinforces that the parent will not take ownership of the problems or consequences caused by their children's bad choices but will gladly love them through solving those problems for themselves and dealing with those consequences.

Two other points beneath this rule are also crucial to understand here. The first is that the most important thing for consultant parents to learn, especially if their children are older, is to neutralize their child's arguing. A parent can do a beautiful job of setting firm limits with an enforceable statement, showing empathy at their child's mistake, and turning the problem back over to the child, and then completely destroy anything positive the child can learn from the interaction by then getting dragged into an argument with their kid. Consultant parents blow in, blow off, and then blow out—they don't blow up!

Our best advice for parents who have reached the blowing-up point is to go completely brain-dead and return to their one-liners. Some of the best are, "I love you too much to argue with you," "I know," and "Nice try!" The conversation could go something like this:

JESSICA: "But Dad, that's not fair!"
DAD: "I know."
JESSICA: "But none of my friends would have to do anything like that!"
DAD: "I know."
JESSICA: "If that is the way you feel, then you just don't love me!"
DAD: "Nice try! You know I will love you no matter what happens."
JESSICA: "Ugh! I can't talk to you! You are so five-minutes-ago! None of my friends has a parent like you!"
DAD: "I know, it must be a bummer to have a father like me sometimes, but you know what? I love you too much to argue with you. We should discuss this when both of us are less emotional about it."

The second point is that consequences can, and often should, be delayed. There is nothing wrong with saying something like, "Uh-oh! I am going to have to do something about that, but not right now. I am busy with something else. I will get back to you on that. Try not to worry about it." This is especially good if you are in the car and truly can't do anything about it at the moment, if you are out in public, or if you simply can't think of anything to do about it. It is okay to take some time and call a friend, teacher, advisor, or minister to get some good ideas about how to respond. Perhaps you could return to this book or check our Love and Logic website at www.loveandlogic.com for ideas.

Many people have been taught that the best time to respond is immediately because they feel the impact will be lost if time passes. But haven't you ever heard about a two-year-old remembering a promise made a week ago about getting something she wanted the next time Mommy took her to the store? Don't worry! Your kids have a good memory too. And often in the time between problem and consequence, either they'll find a solution to the problem for themselves, or the perfect consequence will present itself to you so that the children will get optimal learning out of the situation!

The key is to keep the ball in the kid's court and model taking care of yourself. Then, even if the kids think they have gotten away with it, when the consequences come they will be more meaningful because you took the time to find the best response.

Problem, Problem, Who Owns the Problem?

Unfortunately, separating the kids' problems from our problems is not always as cut and dry as we would like. The line between the two often becomes blurred by parental indecision, guilt, insecurity, and our own childhood's authoritarianism. When our guilt or indecision moves us to step into our children's problems, we cater more to our own emotions than to the children's needs. Most kids want us to understand *their* feelings, not soothe our own emotional turmoil by offering them solutions.

LOVE AND LOGIC TIP 12

If It's a Problem for Us, It Should Soon Become a Problem for Them

"Where's Snuggles?" The question from Emily, a seven-year-old girl, was frantic with concern. Emily missed the excited yelping when she got off the bus. She missed the afternoon throw-and-retrieve game. When she investigated further, she found that her dog was nowhere to be found.

"I've taken Snuggles to her new home at Betty's place," Emily's mother said.

"To Betty's house?" asked Emily.

"Right," Mom said. "But there's bad news and good news. The bad news is that Betty is already falling in love with Snuggles and may never want to give her up. The good news is that Betty gave us three days to decide if Snuggles can come back here."

"Snuggles is at Betty's house?" Emily screamed. "Why?"

"Well, frankly," Mom said, "I got tired of seeing Snuggles' ribs showing. I don't like looking at skinny, malnourished dogs that are being abused. Their whining bothers my ears and their ribs disturb my eyeballs, so Snuggles needed a new home."

"B-b-b-but how do I get Snuggles back?" Emily stammered. "Will you take me to Betty's house?"

"You must be kidding," Mom said flatly. "I just took the dog over there. Now I'm supposed to bring her back? Do I look like an idiot?"

So Emily phoned a neighbor who happened to drive near Betty's house on his way to work. (Kids can be very resourceful when they have to be.) Mom had phoned the neighbor earlier in the day to explain what might happen.

"Sure, I'll take you by there on my way to work," the neighbor said. "And I'll pick you and Snuggles up on my way home. You'll have to call Betty and see if you can spend the day at her house."

"Oh, I will," Emily gushed. "I will."

Snuggles is safe at home now—happy, loved, appreciated, and *well fed.* Emily learned an important lesson about responsibility.

We sometimes worry that this approach sounds too tough, taking the pet out of the home with the possibility it may never return. But we also know that life offers much tougher consequences. The message we want to convey to our children is that neglecting responsibilities presents serious consequences. Poor personal health habits, for example, can lead to illness and, ultimately, death. Children need to learn that lesson. The question is this: Will they learn it on goldfish or hamsters or dogs, or on themselves?

This is tough on us. Our guilt nags us; our insecurity bugs us to death. What will our friends think when our son is the jerk of his school? How will we be viewed at church when it's our daughter who never remembers the name of the boy who slew Goliath? How can parents who love their child stand back and watch him or her blow it time and time again without stepping in with help? Our intervention into our children's problems demonstrates a selfish love. We must rise up in a higher love—a love that shows itself in allowing our children to learn on their own.

Standing at her kitchen window, Robin watches son Josh slug neighbor boy Parker, after which Parker, unhurt, flees home in tears. Is this a child's problem? Of course it is. If Robin allows her own emotions to control her reaction, she can rob Josh of the chance to grow in responsibility. For example, if she reacts with embarrassment—"What will people think?"—Josh receives the message that she doesn't care about how *he* feels; she cares only about how others feel. If she is angry and authoritarian—"Don't do that! Apologize to Parker!"—Josh will rebel. Parents who make a child do something their way find that the child tries all the harder to do it his or her way. If she throws up her hands in helplessness—"What will I ever do with you?"—she assumes ownership of the problem. Josh will probably think, *I don't know, but* you *figure it out.*

Each of these possible responses is based on Robin's own emotions. Each denies Josh the chance to tackle his own problem. It would be better for Robin to focus on Josh. She could either say nothing or offer her ear for listening if Josh wants to talk about it. Or if she is so troubled she feels she must express her disapproval, she could say, "Josh, I saw what you did to Parker. Do you approve of that? What would be the right thing to do now? How do you think Parker feels? I hope next time you'll find a better way to solve that kind of problem." Such comments put the burden of resolving the problem as well as the future response on Josh's shoulders.

What should Robin do if Parker's mother, Kelly, comes over spitting nails? How would she keep this Josh's problem? If that happens, it is best for Robin to say, "Well, Kelly, I can understand your being upset. If my son had been hit, I'd be upset too. I think it would be great for you to tell Josh exactly how you feel. In fact, I'll call him down and you can talk to him now."

Robin must emphasize to Kelly that she cannot control her son's behavior when he is away from home but, on the other hand, understands if Parker is angry and wants to hit Josh back. Robin tells Kelly that she will let Josh know that this threat is a distinct possibility and that such consequences would be sad for *him*. Throughout this whole episode, Robin should realize that Kelly may not be helping her son Parker by moving in and taking care of Parker's problems. On the other hand, she also realizes it might help Josh a lot to let him know that the neighbors are upset and will not let him get away with such an act.

Allowing children to solve their own problems presumes an implicit, basic trust that their behavior will change as they learn from their experiences. For example, Josh might learn that hitting another person usually results in bad news for the provocateur.

To repeat: The best solution to any problem lies within the skin of the person who rightfully owns the problem.

5

Setting Limits Through Thinking Words

Rash words are like sword thrusts,
but the tongue of the wise brings healing.
Proverbs 12:18

Love and Logic parenting is a law-and-order philosophy. Just because we recommend that parents shy away from issuing orders and imposing their solutions on their kids' problems does not mean we give license to all sorts of misbehavior. Nothing could be further from the truth. Neither of us is in any way soft on misbehavior.

True, we allow our kids to mess up, and we don't drive home the lesson of their misdeeds with our words. We are slow to lecture; we never actually tell our kids what they have just learned. We believe telling our kids what to think is counterproductive. We can give them guidance (more on that in subsequent chapters), but they must think for themselves. Making enforceable statements and giving choices forces that thinking back on them.

LOVE AND LOGIC TIP 13

Using Love and Logic with Toddlers

Parenting with Love and Logic involves setting strong limits and boundaries in toddlerhood. Not only do limits protect our children from harmful situations, they also allow us to model good adult behavior by caring for ourselves. Let's look at a couple of examples.

Two toddlers, "Thoughtful" and "Thug," want to be picked up. They raise their hands and scream demandingly at their parents. Thug's parents pick him up. In essence, they say, "Be obnoxious with me and you'll get your way." However, when Thoughtful raises her hands and screams, her father says, without anger or sarcasm, "Thoughtful, why don't you lie down on the linoleum? I can't pick you up when you act like that." Thoughtful learns right away to say, as politely as possible, "Daddy, will you please pick me up?"

All infants at about six months discover their pitching arm and attempt to train their mothers to fetch as the baby bottle first falls off the high-chair tray and is then thrown by the baby. Each mom plays fetch in her own unique manner. Some moms are one-bottle retrievers; most are three-to-four-bottle retrievers. Some are more enjoyable and will retrieve over and over, at least twice or three times every meal. From a baby's point of view, the most fun are the sighing or noisy retrievers: "Will you *please* quit throwing your milk bottle off the tray?" Some retrievers are quiet but lovingly say, in their actions, "You can choose to throw the bottle once every meal and I'll pick it up, and then you have chosen to save your arm for the next meal." The game is a lot shorter and less fun for the pitcher, but the retriever leads a happier life, and soon the bottle isn't pitched at all.

The boundaries we set for our children are in reality the boundaries we set for ourselves. The more squishy and indecisive we are about our own boundaries, the more soggy and inconsistent we are about the limits we set for our toddlers.

The earlier they start, the better. When our children leave our care, we want them to be so good at thinking, that they can face the bigger problems and the daily hassles of life with competence and good sense.

So if we don't order our kids around, how *do* we talk to them? How do we set limits on their behavior without telling them what to do? Limits are crucial to Love and Logic parenting. Our kids need the security in which they can begin making those all-important decisions. They have to know the boundaries.

Building Walls That Don't Crumble

Imagine yourself plopped down on a chair in a strange, totally dark environment. You can't see your hand in front of your face. Your only security is the chair. You don't know if you're on a cliff, in a cave, or in a room. Eventually, you muster enough nerve to move away from the chair and check your immediate surroundings. You find four solid walls. What a relief! Now you feel safe enough to begin exploring the rest of the room, knowing that you won't fall off the edge. But what if the walls crumbled when you tested them? You would move quickly back to your chair for security. And there you would stay. Your entire environment is mysterious and threatening.

Now imagine what it is like for newborn babies. They pop out of the cozy, comfortable, familiar surroundings of the womb into a totally unknown, alien world. They seek limits on their behavior; they feel secure when they know what they can and cannot do.

From the time our kids are infants, we set limits for them—limits that put boundaries around their behavior. How fast do we bolt from our interrupted deep sleep to tend to Wailing Will in his crib? Do we permit little Abbey to wage baby food war from the high chair? Is Nate allowed to slap Mommy when he's mad? Can Paige make our every shopping expedition a walk on the wild side? Some parents build walls in the form of firm limits for their children; others leave their kids to feel insecure and afraid by providing few limits, or limits that crumble easily.

Foster once counseled a young mother whose son Graham was a walking slot machine. The boy ate coins—pennies, nickels, dimes, not many quarters, and *no* half dollars. She was thankful for that, but it was still a problem. Graham would start to swallow a nickel, and Mom would make like a Samoan pearl diver trying to dig it out. "I tell him not to, but I can't make him stop," she complained. "What am I going to do?"

Foster found out during their conversation that they lived on a busy Denver thoroughfare, so he asked the mom, "Does Graham run out onto Wadsworth Boulevard?"

The mom said, "Well, of course not. On *that* I mean business."

One limit was responded to with noise and frustration, the other in a firm, no-nonsense manner. Graham knew playing in traffic was a no-no, but when it came to eating coins, *bon appetit*. Now that one was *fun*!

Kids seem most secure around parents who are strong, who don't allow the limits they place on their kids to crumble. Children lose respect for adults who cannot set limits and make them stick. Kids who misbehave without having to face the consequences become brats.

Children lucky enough to have limits placed on them in loving ways become secure enough to not only deal effectively with their own emotions but also form satisfying relationships with others. These limits allow children to develop self-confidence. As a result, these children are easier to teach, they spend less time misbehaving, and they grow up to be responsible adults. When we don't provide firm limits, our kids suffer from low self-esteem. And when they have low self-esteem, they behave accordingly.

LOVE AND LOGIC TIP 14

Oh, the Rationalizations We Weave for Misbehavior

Catherine and Jeremy have problems with their two children, but Catherine admits she has a lot more problem with their behavior than Jeremy does. But she explains, "That's because I'm around them all the time."

The amazing thing is that Jeremy nods his agreement. "That's right. They mind me, but Catherine's around them all the time."

Wow! Do you think Catherine would accept that response from a teacher if one of the third-grade classes were out of control? "Well, of course, the class is a real mess, but I've had them all semester!" That sort of thinking also wouldn't work for the average residential treatment center or for a first sergeant leading basic training: "I have trouble with all the recruits, but, heck, I've been around them for the entire six weeks!"

Parents' guilt probably plays a larger role than most of us realize. Guilt excuses the child's misbehavior: "If I were a better parent, they wouldn't be acting this way," or "If it weren't for our divorce, they wouldn't be so difficult," or "I'm a working mom, and I don't give Jacob enough time, so it's no wonder he's out of control. Poor little latchkey kid." This excusing of irresponsible and destructive behavior because children have somehow been wronged can be carried to ridiculous extremes. "Perhaps if the boys hadn't been ostracized and if other children hadn't made fun of them, they wouldn't have taken the guns to school."

Love and Logic parents give a far different message: "Times can be real tough, and you have the opportunity to learn from them. If anyone can cope with difficulties, it's you. I bet you are very proud of yourself." The Love and Logic single working mom doesn't feel guilty and gives no apology. Her working is an opportunity for her children to grow: "You guys are so lucky I provide for you. You are so lucky to have me for a mom, and I'm lucky to have you. And I expect you will choose to be a big help to me. Thanks!"

How to Talk to a Child

For many parents, setting limits means issuing commands and backing up those limits with more commands spiced with sternness and anger. They figure every time they say something to their kids, they're setting limits, and the louder their voice gets and the more often they repeat it, the firmer the limits become. They may get results with their orders, but they're setting their kids up for a fight (against them) and doing them a great disservice at the same time.

You've probably noticed that there's something different in how Love and Logic parents talk to kids. We're always asking questions. We're always offering choices. We don't tell our kids what to do, but we put the burden of decision making on their shoulders. As they grow older, we don't tell them what the limits are; we establish limits by offering choices.

LOVE AND LOGIC TIP 15

Fighting Words and Thinking Words

Another way to think of enforceable statements is that they are words that make kids think for themselves. Observe the difference between some fighting and thinking words:[4]

Child says something loud and unkind to the parents.
FIGHTING WORDS: "Don't you talk to me in that tone of voice!"
THINKING WORDS: "You sound upset. I'll be glad to listen when your voice is as soft as mine is."

Child is dawdling with her homework.
FIGHTING WORDS: "You get to work on your studying!"
THINKING WORDS: "Feel free to join us for some television when your studying is done."

Two kids are fighting.
FIGHTING WORDS: "Be nice to each other. Quit fighting."
THINKING WORDS: "You guys are welcome to come back as soon as you work that out."

Child won't do his chores.
FIGHTING WORDS: "I want that lawn cut now!"
THINKING WORDS: "I'll take you to your soccer game as soon as the lawn is cut."

Love and Logic parents insist on respect and obedience, just as command-oriented parents do. But when Love and Logic parents talk to their children, they take a different approach. Instead of the fighting words of command-oriented parents, they use thinking words.

Thinking words—used in question form and expressed in enforceable statements—are one of the keys to parenting with Love and Logic. They place the responsibility for thinking and decision making on the children. They help kids do exactly what we want them to do—think—as much as possible.

Children learn better from what they tell themselves than from what we tell them. They may do what we order them to do, but their motivation for obedience comes from a voice other than their own: ours. Kids believe something that comes from inside their own heads. When they choose an option, they do the thinking, they make the choice, and the lesson sticks. That's why, from early childhood on, parents must always be asking thinking questions:

- "Would you rather carry your coat or wear it?"
- "Would you rather put your boots on now or in the car?"
- "Would you rather play nicely in front of the television or be noisy in your room?"

We don't use fighting words:

- "You put that coat on now!"
- "Because I said put your boots on, that's why! It's snowing outside."
- "I'm trying to watch this football game, so be quiet!"

The difference between thinking words and fighting words may be subtle; after all, the limit in each case is the same, but the child's reaction is usually different. Kids fight against commands. They see an implied threat in them. When we tell them to do something, they see our words as an attempt to take control of the situation. Anytime we usurp more control, it means that they have less control. They exert themselves to regain the control they see slipping away.

The Threat Cycle

The temptation is oh so great. We desperately want to assail our kids with commands and threats to limit their behavior. The reasons are simple:

1. Using threats doesn't make us feel like the wimp we feel like if we whimper, cry, beg, or plead with our kids.
2. Threats sometimes work.

In Jim's early years as a teacher, he frequently used threats to motivate students to do their work. To one student, he would say, "You get that work done or you're not going to lunch," and the kid's pencil became an instantaneous cyclone of activity. To another he would say the same thing, and the kid would say, "Who cares?" Some kids respond to threats, and some don't. They may do as they're told, but they're angry with the person who gave the order. Or they may perform the task in a way that is unsatisfactory simply to regain some of the control they had taken from them. In either case, they're breaking the limit we're trying to set.

In fact, what really started us on the Love and Logic quest back in the 1970s was an incident that happened to some local teens. Two girls were caught shoplifting, and both sets of parents handed down the same sets of consequences, but the results were dramatically different! One of the girls saw her parents as being mean, but the other saw her parents as just trying to help her prepare for the real world. When we asked ourselves what the difference had been, we had to admit we had no idea. We also realized that if we could find out, it would give us some wonderful insight to share with parents to make life a lot better for them and their kids. Over the next few years, we searched and searched and couldn't find the answer in books or seminars. We found it by watching the really effective parents and analyzing what they did and how they did it! Then we went to psychological research to help explain it. We've summed up our findings in the two rules of Love and Logic we discussed in the previous chapter, and it all started with using thinking words and enforceable statements.

LOVE AND LOGIC TIP 16

Eat Nicely Here, or Play on the Floor

Dinnertime with two-year-old Lukas. Mommy and Daddy are talking over the day's events and listening to the little tyke's new words and experiences. A cozy scene for family bonding and love, right? That's how Mom and Dad see it, but Lukas has different ideas.

First the bread crust is hurled into Dad's soup, splashing the Christmas tie. Then the little fists are sledgehammering the sliced-up wieners on his tray. Next he's on his feet trying to climb out the back of the high chair. Then the top is off his safety cup, and he's anointing Fido with milk, all of which is punctuated with intermittent bloodcurdling screams like those from shoppers at the after-Thanksgiving Day sale at Wal-Mart.

Mom and Dad have a problem. They must convince this child that such dinner behavior is unacceptable. They must set limits. They could slap his little hands, grab his little shoulders, and peer directly into his little eyes while saying, "Lukas, eat nice or Daddy spanks." And Lukas would show them just how strong his little lungs are. Or they could say, "Lukas, would you like to eat nicely in the chair, or would you like to play on the floor?" Notice that the parents do not ask Lukas to "play nicely" on the floor. We can't make a child play nicely on the floor, but we can help him to eat nicely. One thing is under our control; the other is not.

Fighting words, or enforceable, thinking words. With fighting words, Mom and Dad have done all of the thinking, and the meal is chaos. With the thinking words, they let Lukas do some thinking, and order is restored. The parents have shown Lukas how they make themselves happy by taking care of themselves, and Lukas can decide about his own happiness.

If Lukas chooses the floor, he may learn soon enough that it's a long, hunger-filled time until breakfast. Naturally, when providing such options as waiting until breakfast, the average child will make the rest of the night as miserable as possible. Older children will whine that they are hungry, and younger children will keep parents up with wails of unhappiness. Wise parents show compassion, stick to their guns, and show minimal frustration in spite of the child's best attempt to provoke it.

On the other hand, after an hour or so, Lukas may have already learned his lesson and be ready to sit and eat nicely. However it's handled, the child needs to learn what all happy adults know: "If you are very difficult to be around, there's a chance it will be harder to get food in life!" All this is accomplished with no anger, threats, or fighting words.

Too bad about the Christmas tie.

Passive-Aggressive Behavior

When children are commanded to do something they don't like, they often respond with passive-aggressive behavior. Kids know they must comply with the order or else reap punishment. They channel their anger in a way that will hurt their parents—so subtly that the parents don't know they're being hurt. They'll make it sting sharply enough so that those parents will think twice before giving that order again.

Becca was assigned to do the dishes—something she ranked on her happy-meter right up there with letting dentists drill her teeth. She used every conceivable trick to get out of it. Sometimes she was able to put it off past her bedtime. Then, all of a sudden, she became very mature about her need for the good old eight hours a night: "You're always telling me I need my sleep," she'd say. "I'll do them in the morning." Of course, when morning came, she was running late and had to rush for the bus. There the dishes sat, still unwashed. Eventually, Mom did them because they were stinking up the kitchen.

But Mom decided to get tough one night and said to Becca, "I want those dishes washed now! I'm tired of you wasting all evening in front of that television while those dishes sit there."

"Oh, all right," Becca replied, "I'll do it." She walked to the sink and washed with such enthusiasm and gusto that she "accidentally" dropped one of Mom's best glasses. It shattered on the floor. "Oh, I'm sorry, Mom," she said when Mom raced into the room. "I was trying so hard. I wanted to do a good job." Mom is between a rock and a hard place. How could Mom punish a girl who was trying so hard?

Becca's passive-aggressive behavior told her mom an important message: *You'll think twice before you make me do the dishes again.* Mom might conclude, "What's the use? It's easier to do it myself than to go through all this."

Passive-Resistive Behavior

When kids react to parental demands with passive-resistive behavior, they resist without telling the parent they are resisting. The resistance is in their actions, not their words. For example, when a parent tells a child to do something, the child responds by claiming he or she forgot the request or with less-than-instantaneous obedience.

One of Brandon's teachers ordered, "Get down the hall to your class, young man, and get there right away." Brandon "got" down the hall, all right, but his movement was imperceptible to the human eye.

The teacher said, "Hurry up, Brandon."

"Hey, I'm going," Brandon replied. "I'm doing what you told me. How come you're always on my case?" Brandon was attempting to wrest back some control of the situation. He was fighting. *I'll go,* he said inside. *But I won't go your way—I'll go my way.*

A sure sign of passive-resistant behavior in children is prolonged parental frustration. Certainly, parents may be frustrated without having passive-resistant children, but all passive-resistant children have frustrated parents.

In the sections that follow, we will discuss some techniques that Love and Logic parents use to decrease parental frustration and children's noncompliance. We'll discover various options that Becca's mom or Brandon's teacher could have used.

We'd Rather They Think Than Fight

Fighting words invite disobedience. When we use them, we draw a line in the sand and dare our kids to cross it. They will fight the limits we impose when we use fighting words. Fighting words include three types of commands:

1. Telling our kids what to do—"You get to work on that lawn right now."
2. Telling our kids what we will not allow—"You're not going to talk to me that way!"
3. Telling our kids what we won't do for them—"I'm not letting you out of this house until you clean the living room."

When we issue such commands we are calling our kids to battle, and in many cases these are battles we cannot win. Why not bypass these hassles and make our words ones that cannot be fought? Why not steer away from commands? Limits can be set much more effectively when we're not fighting with our kids. It has been clinically proven that kids who are thinking cannot fight us at the same time.

Love and Logic parents make statements with enforceable thinking words, telling their kids:

- What we will allow—"Feel free to join us for your next meal as soon as the lawn is mowed."
- What we will do—"I'll be glad to read you a story as soon as you've finished your bath."
- What we will provide—"You may eat what is served, or you may wait and see if the next meal appeals to you more."

Our kids have little chance to fight these statements. They're too busy thinking about the choices they have been given and the consequences that may result from their choice.

LOVE AND LOGIC TIP 17

Let Your "Yes" Be Yes, and Your "No" Be Yes Too

The word *no* is one of the biggest fighting words in the parental arsenal of commands. It is a child's call to arms, a shot across his bow. Kids hear it far too often. In fact, parents of two-year-olds are known to say "no"—in some form or other—77 percent of the time. Children gradually tire of hearing it. In fact, they hear it so much that the first word many children learn to say is "no" and variations of it. When kids hear "no," half the time they ignore it. They hear it so much that sometimes they think it means "maybe," and other times they think it really means "yes."

The rule with "no" is that we use it as seldom as possible. But when we use it, we mean business. All of the other times we are tempted to use "no," we can avoid a fight by replacing "no" with a "yes" to something else. In this way, we use thinking words instead of fighting words, and we establish the behavior we want. Compare the two:

FIGHTING WORDS: "No, you can't go out to play until you practice your lessons."
THINKING WORDS: "Yes, you may go out to play as soon as you practice your lessons."

FIGHTING WORDS: "No, you can't watch television until your chores are done."
THINKING WORDS: "Yes, you may watch television as soon as your chores are done."

By using thinking words, we are able to set limits on our children's behavior without telling them what to do. For instance, if we want the lawn mowed before they eat their next meal, we set that limit by offering them a choice: of mowing the lawn and eating, or of not doing the lawn and not eating.

Now, when offered such choices, our children will probably say, "That's not fair! Why should I have to take either of those choices?" The answer lies in the fact that our choices must always make "real world" sense (we'll explore this more in chapter 6). So we would lovingly say to our child, "Well, honey, that's the way the world works for me. First I get my job done, then I get paid, and then I eat. If it's good enough for me, who do you suppose I think it's also good enough for?" The child will always answer, a little dejectedly but insightfully, "Me." And we always respond with, "Good thinking." When we give our children the right to make decisions, there is no anger for them to rebel against. Nobody's doing their thinking for them, and the limit is established.

Finally, let's just admit it: When we ourselves make requests of others and we get a "yes" answer, it makes our heart sing and we have a positive feeling about the other party. "Yes" is just more fun to say than "no" if we are healthy and don't get a kick out of controlling others. Loving parents often feel they must say "no" to requests that they *do* something they don't think is in the child's best interest: buy candy, buy toys, provide a new car, and so on. Love and Logic parents who encourage responsibility early are less likely to get into the yes-or-no hassle:

CHILD: "Can I have (candy, prom dress, car)?"
MOM: "Honey, if anyone deserves that (candy, prom dress, car), it's you. Buy it!"
CHILD: "I don't have the money."
MOM: "Sorry about that. It's like that a lot for me too. I guess then you won't buy it."

Mean What You Say, and Say What You Mean

Just as quickly as kids learn the limits, they'll test them. In fact, they need to test them in order to assure themselves that the limits are firm enough to provide the needed security. They *need* to find out if we mean what we say—if we're going to stand firm on our word or not. They have to discover if the walls are real or if they will crumble when they are tested.

Most children seem to have their own special testing routine. Some use anger or guilt, some are sneaky, and others feign forgetfulness as a means of testing parental resolve. They never seem to say, "Thanks, Dad, I feel a lot more secure now that I know you mean what you say. I appreciate your loving me enough to set these limits." Instead, they pout, complain, stomp around, run to their rooms, whine, or talk back. Kids are not above laying guilt trips on us either. If we tell them to get the job done before they next eat, they'll respond with, "Imagine being raised by a dad who doesn't even let me eat around this place!"

Using Love and Logic doesn't mean any of this will go away; the fact is that it often increases. Kids would prefer you went back to your old methods than continue as things are now. However, Love and Logic parents are ready for the siege and know how to come through it with everyone the better for the experience. While kids will do anything to make us back off, we must stand firm. After all, the limit that was imposed was the children's choice. Of course they're hungry if they decided to put off their next meal because they didn't mow the lawn. That hunger is the natural consequence of their action. If you don't work, you don't eat. We are certainly empathetic with their hunger. We know how it feels to miss a meal, and we tell them so in all kindness and understanding: "It is a bummer to miss a meal. Any of us would feel hungry. But, boy, do I ever enjoy the next meal."

If we relent, we demolish the meaning of those consequences. We set up a crumbling limit for our children. If we get angry at them for the choice they made or if we rail into them with an "I-told-you-so," we also present a crumbling limit. Those children then have ample reason to direct their anger toward their parents instead of themselves.

Using enforceable thinking words, giving choices, displaying no anger—these are the ingredients for establishing firm limits with our kids.

6

Gaining Control Through Choices

Hear, my child, and accept my words,
that the years of your life may be many.
Proverbs 4:10

"Calling Garrett to dinner is like calling the cat," Natalie said. "He doesn't even flinch when I talk to him. He spends all his time at his computer. One night, I said to him, 'Come to dinner,' and do you think he came? He never even looked up. So I said it louder. Again nothing happened. So I said, 'I mean it!' Garrett just kept punching away. I am so frustrated! How can I be a good mother if I can't make my kid do what I want him to do, when I want him to do it?"

Many of us share Natalie's frustration and her concept of parenting. We don't feel like good parents unless we can run our kids around like little robots. It all boils down to control. We want to control our children. We want them to do what we want them to do, when we want them to do it. At times, our kids fight us with a passion. Before we know it, we're locked into a control struggle.

How much easier it would have been for Natalie to use thinking words, whispered into her son's ear: "We'll be serving dinner for the next twenty minutes, and we'd love to have you join us because we love eating with you. We hope you make it. But if not, just catch us at breakfast." But no, Natalie couldn't do that, nor can many of us. When we do it, we don't feel as if we're in control.

Parenting Just Gets More and More Curious

Control is a curious thing. The more we give away, the more we gain. Parents who attempt to take all the control from their children end up losing the control they sought to begin with. These parents invite their children to fight to get control back. In the battle for control, we should never take any more than we absolutely must have, and we must always cut our kids in on the action. When we do that, we put them in control on our terms. We need to set the limits, but then we must give our children control of how they operate within those limits.

This battle for control begins early in life. From infancy on, children live a drama of gaining responsibility and control over their own lives. Little Madeline wants to make decisions; she wants to think for herself.

Giving even the smallest children a certain amount of freedom and control over their lives instills in them the sense of responsibility and maturity we want them to have. Independence helps children learn about the real world as their wisdom grows from the results of their decisions.

However, there is a downside: We can give our kids too much control, and kids with too much control are not pleasant to be around. In fact, they don't even like to be around themselves. They're brats. These children need to be controlled; their behavior indicates they'd be happier if they were controlled. Yet they demand more control with their pouts and tantrums. Control is power. Having had at least some degree of control very early in life, they always seek more.

LOVE AND LOGIC TIP 18
You'll Do What I Tell You to Do

Amy, the mother of twelve-year-old Brooke, parents in the "Do what I tell you to do" style. Amy thinks she should be in control of everything in her daughter's life. She controls when Brooke gets up, when she goes to bed, what kinds of clothes she wears, who her friends are supposed to be, what grades she is supposed to get, and how much television she watches.

Parents like Amy, when they come home from a night out, don't rush to hug their kids and say, "We missed you." They run to the television set and hug *it* to see if it's still warm from being on when it was supposed to be off! Kids will take this stuff for a while, but eventually they shake off this blanketlike control. One day Brooke said to herself, *Mom is getting out of line. It's about time to reel her in. Maybe it's time for her to get a C on the report card.* Brooke received the C, and Amy came unglued. She ranted, raved, grounded, withheld, lectured, yelled at the teachers, and recruited her husband to deliver his "Get good grades now or you'll never cut it in college" speech. Brooke sat back and thought, *You haven't seen anything yet. Wait until Mom gets an F.*

Poor Amy. She has yet to discover that kids get report cards, parents don't. Amy cannot make her daughter learn. Amy actually loses control over Brooke with every ounce of effort she pours into her quest for controlling her. It's one of the many battles Amy, and all parents, will eventually lose.

The battles we can't win are those that center on children's brain activity. If kids can hook us into trying to make them talk, think, learn, go to sleep at a certain time, or like certain foods, they've got us. We'll never win those battles, and moreover, we'll expend needed energy fighting them—energy that can be effectively channeled into battles we *can* win.

When parents pull in the reins, these children resist and are filled with anger. Kids who start with too much power force us to tighten the limits around them, and that makes them angry. Adults are no different. When control in some area of life is reduced, we also react with anger. We feel that what is rightfully ours has been stripped away.

The Right Dose of Control

What, then, is the right amount of control to give children? Psychologist Sylvia B. Rimm, PhD, says people of all ages compare the amount of control they have in a relationship to only the amount of control they used to have—not to the amount they feel they should have. When more control is allotted with time, people are satisfied; when control is cut back, people are angry. Thus, children who grow up with parents who dole out control in increasing amounts are usually satisfied with the level of control. It's always more than it used to be.[5]

Rimm's analysis is called the "V" of love. The sides of the "V" represent firm limits within which the child may make decisions and live with the consequences. The bottom of the "V" represents birth, while the top represents the time when the child leaves home for adult life.

In the "V" of love, we offer more and more freedom as the years go by. Unfortunately, many parents do the opposite (the inverted "V"). They grant many privileges when the children are young and then take control away from their kids as they grow older. The result is unhappy children.

When kids are very little, Love and Logic parents will give away control in certain areas. While giving the tyke a bath, the Love and

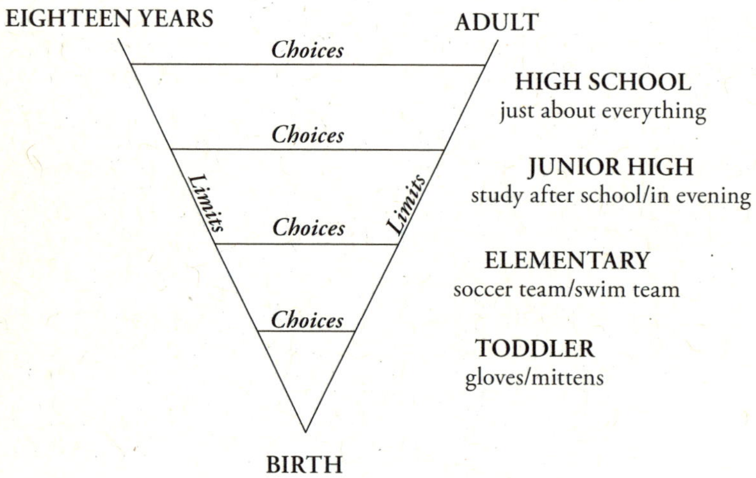

"V" of Love

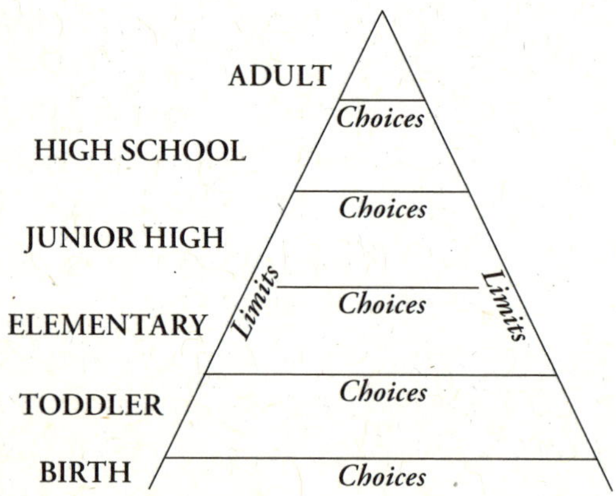

Inverted "V"

Logic dad will say, "Do you want to get out of the tub now, or do you want to stay in a few more minutes?" Dad doesn't need that control. Or at the table, Mom might say, "Have you had enough milk, or would you like some more?" Mom gives that control to the child. Thus, toddlers make decisions about things like chocolate or white milk, ten-year-olds decide how to spend their allowances, and seventeen-year-olds make decisions on nearly every aspect of their lives. The children gain more control over their lives as time goes on.

Unfortunately, many parents invert the "V". They treat their kids like miniature adults right from the start, with all the privileges of adulthood granted immediately at birth. These children soon become tyrants. Their parents don't control them; they control their parents, holding them hostage with temper tantrums and pouts. More tragically, many children who begin life with too much power eventually lead unhappy lives as they grow older. Misbehavior early in life forces parents to clamp down on them, resulting in anger and rebellion as rights and privileges are forcibly withdrawn. These unhappy youngsters are forever crying, "Life's not fair! You're always treating me like a child."

Waging a Winnable War with Choices

There are some areas of our children's lives that remain beyond our control and are best avoided. If we exert our will over children in these areas, we are destined to fail. Any parent who has pleaded, cajoled, bribed, threatened, contorted his face grotesquely, or done headstands trying to make a little tyke talk for relatives already knows about these sorts of control battles. Vince isn't going to talk unless *he* wants to. The same goes for the battle of the pureed vegetables. We can force-feed them down Lily's little gullet all we want, but if she doesn't want to eat them, back out they come. And we lose. Ditto at the other end of the gastrointestinal tract. We may demand that our children do their dirty work on the potty chair, but before we know it, they're over in the corner of the family room with faces sporting an ominous flushed look.

These are battles we can't win with commands. They pertain to what children learn, think, and eat; when they go to bed or the bathroom; and so forth. In each, children fight tenaciously to win, and when we get involved in these battles, we invariably lose. We influence our children in these areas only by modeling. We model how much we like *our* food at the table. We talk, in self-referenced comments, about how good it makes us feel to clean up *our* plate, to eat *our* vegetables. But every time we issue demands, we invite a fight, and eventually we lose.

The secret to establishing control is to concentrate on fighting battles that we know we can win. That means we must select the issues very carefully. We must pick areas where we *do* have control over our kids. Then we must offer choices in those areas.

We may not be able to make Emma eat when she's at the table—that's an unwinnable battle—but we can control whether she's at the table or not. We may not be able to control when Justin does his chores, but we can make sure he does them before he eats his next meal. We may not be able to control the disrespectful words that pop out of Alyssa's mouth, but we can make sure she doesn't use them in our presence—we send her away until she can speak reasonably with us.[6]

We cannot afford to demand blind obedience to our every wish. When faced with such demands, kids dig in their heels and hold out for their own values—and that's a control battle we'll lose every time.

LOVE AND LOGIC TIP 19
Three Rules for Control Battles

1. Avoid a control battle at all costs.
2. If you're going to get into one, win at all costs.
3. Pick the issue carefully. Whenever a control battle is lost, it's because the issue was not chosen carefully.

Choices Change Everything

Winnable war is waged through choices, not demands. Choices change the entire complexion of the control struggle. They allow us to give away the control we don't need and gain the control we do. With choices, kids have no demands to react against, and the control we need is established.

One parent said, "As soon as I give my three-year-old a choice, everything changes. It works every time. I see a complete personality change in Gabrielle when she has a choice—when I change my words from fighting words to thinking words. I'm still setting the limit, and I'm still getting what I want, but I'm eliminating the fighting."

Why Choices Work

One reason choices work is that they create situations in which children are forced to think. Kids are given options to ponder, courses of action to choose. They must decide. Second, choices provide opportunities for children to make mistakes and learn from the consequences. With every wrong choice the children make, the punishment comes not from us but from the world around them. Then children don't get angry at us; they get angry at themselves.

Another reason choices work is because they help us avoid getting into control battles with our children. Finally, choices provide our children with opportunities to hear that we trust their thinking abilities, thus building their self-confidence and the relationship between us and them.

Dealing with choices and being held responsible for their own decisions prepare youngsters for the lifetime of decision making that awaits them in adulthood. However, parents should offer choices only when they are willing to ensure that their children are forced to live with the consequences.

Picking Fights and Losing Battles

Are some kids born stubborn, or do they become that way as a result of the way they are raised? Well, the answer is yes. Some children, as a condition of inborn temperament, are less cooperative and more prone to resisting being told what to do. And some kids, as a result of how they are raised, become more and more defiant and stubborn as they grow older.

The question is, "Is there a way we can get better cooperation from our kids regardless of how strong-willed they were born?" Yes, there is a way. A small change in the way we talk can result in much better cooperation, fewer fights, fewer temper tantrums, less need for disciplinary action, less hate, and more loving relationships. Great bosses and leaders rely on what we are about to talk about. Great teachers use this technique every day.

Don't Set Yourself Up to Lose

Let's work backward on this. We will study a situation in which a teacher creates a minor disaster in her classroom. Her attempts to control a situation result in a blowup by the student, creating a need for other professionals to be involved. Then we will look at how this could have been avoided in the first place. Once we have done this, we will take a look at the use of this technique in our own homes with our own children:

TEACHER: (speaking from across the room) "Megan, why are you moving your chair? You don't need to do that. Move it back to where it was!"

MEGAN: "Brittany is going to help me."

TEACHER: "You don't need her help. Now, move your chair back to where it was!"

MEGAN: "But I need help on this."

TEACHER: "Move that chair or you're going to get sent to the recovery room."

MEGAN: "I don't have to. You can't tell me what to do. You're not my mother!"

At this point, the situation deteriorated. Megan was ordered to leave the room. She refused and was threatened with disciplinary action. Hearing this, she ran screaming out of the room, and other professionals were drawn into the situation.

A "Nobody Loses" Approach

Here is another approach to the very same situation. No battle line is drawn. Regardless of how the child reacts, she is actually obeying the adult's request. Both the dignity of the adult and the dignity of the child can be maintained. Disciplinary action to help Megan learn the wisdom of cooperating with the teacher can be provided at a later time if necessary:

TEACHER: (walking up to the student and whispering) "Megan, I need you to move your chair back. Would you consider doing that for me? Thank you." (The word *consider* takes away any threat and eliminates the opportunity for Megan to be defiant.)

MEGAN: "But I want Brittany to help me."

TEACHER: (still whispering) "I'm sure that's true, and I'd like you to consider moving."

MEGAN: "No. I don't have to."

TEACHER: (still whispering) "Thanks for considering it. Do you really think that it's wise to refuse when I ask in a nice way? Personally, I don't think that's a wise decision. We'll talk about that later." (The teacher walks away, and Megan remains where she is, provided she does not create a disturbance.)

Because Megan was not ordered to move, she has already complied with the teacher's request. She was not told to move, only to consider moving. Nobody has lost a battle at this point. The other students are not aware of the problem, and the teacher's authority has not been challenged in front of the group. Megan's teacher now has the time to figure out how to deal with Megan's lack of cooperation. If discipline is necessary, it can be done in private.

Applying This Technique to Parenting

How many parents do you know who set themselves up for the same kind of battles by barking orders that may not be enforceable at the time? This can lead to deadly results. Children who recognize that they can defy their parents become increasingly insecure and prone to test limits. Each time a parental request can be ignored or defied, the authority of the parent is reduced in the eyes of the children. It does not take long before these kids think, *I don't have to do anything my parent says.*

It is important to remember that Love and Logic parents are not permissive. Even though they treat their children with dignity and seldom bark orders, they expect that their wishes and requests will be honored. Their children believe in the old saying "Your wish is my command." Children who live in Love and Logic homes have learned through experience that everybody wins when they are cooperative. Now, have these kids ever tested authority? Sure they have. How else did they learn that defiance doesn't pay?

Just like the teacher in the second scenario, parents can set themselves up to be winners as authority figures by using some of the following "Thinking Word Requests" instead of "Fighting Word Demands":

FIGHTING WORD DEMAND: "Take out the trash, and do it now!"
THINKING WORD REQUEST: "I'd appreciate your taking out the trash before bedtime. Thanks."
FIGHTING WORD DEMAND: "Don't you talk to me that way! You go to your room!"
THINKING WORD REQUEST: "Would you mind taking those words to your room? Thank you."
FIGHTING WORD DEMAND: "You come here right now!"
THINKING WORD REQUEST: "Hey, would you mind coming here? Thank you."
FIGHTING WORD DEMAND: "Go help your little sister. Do it now. I mean it!"
THINKING WORD REQUEST: "Would you mind helping your sister now? I'd appreciate it."

Some readers might consider these "Thinking Word Requests" as showing no authority at all. In fact, some readers might even say, "What a wimpy way to talk. How is any authority maintained when you speak so nicely to kids?" Our answer is, "Don't be so quick to judge."

Let's take one of these examples and follow it through to show how kids can learn that it is always best to comply when parents ask in a nice way:

MOM: "Would you mind taking those words to your room? Thank you."
SON: "No! I don't have to."
MOM: "Did I ask in a nice way?"
SON: "Yeah, so what? I'm not leaving!"
MOM: "Not wise, son. I am learning a lot from this."

Mom walks off and allows her son to temporarily believe he has won the battle. However, he will learn later about the foolishness of his decision. The following day he asks his mom to take him across town to his soccer game and discovers the results of being uncooperative:

SON: "Mom, will you take me to my game? Mrs. Howarth can't drive today."
MOM: "I don't know. Did you ask in a nice way?"
SON: "Sure. What's this all about?"
MOM: "Yesterday I learned from you that asking in a nice way doesn't get the job done. Remember that little episode when I asked, in a nice way, for you to go to your room? What did you teach me at that time?"
SON: "I don't know."
MOM: "You taught me that asking in a nice way doesn't mean all that much. I'd appreciate your giving that some thought. And some day when I feel better about your level of cooperation, I'll be glad to help out."

This brave mom did this expecting her son to start begging, complaining, grumbling, and laying on guilt, which of course he did! You probably wonder, *Did she give in and drive him to his game after hearing his begging and complaining? Did she ask, "Now, have you learned your lesson?"* Absolutely not! His angry behavior proved to her that she needed to provide this important lesson for her son. Think about this. Do kids learn best from hearing about consequences, or do they learn best from experiencing them?

The Bad Boy in Burger King: A Case Study on Winning a Control Battle

How, then, do we take control of a situation when our children are determined to battle us every step of the way? The following story sheds light on waging a winnable war with kids.

Six-year-old Aidan was a master at goading his folks into unwinnable control battles. Picture him seated in a fast-food restaurant booth with Mom and Dad. They are all slurping up the last of their soft drinks and gathering their things to leave for some shopping before the mall closes. All except for Aidan. He's blowing bubbles through his Coke straw, he's playing airplane with his French fries, and his teeth have no more than nibbled the edges of his hamburger bun.

Mom, her face resembling a Technicolor explosion, says through gritted teeth, "Hurry up with that thing! We've got shopping to do." Aidan responds by buzzing his hamburger with a fry. He's heavy into everything but eating. Now Dad jumps into the fray: "Can't you do something with that kid?" he asks his wife. "The stores will be closed by the time we get out of here." Mom grabs Aidan's burger and tries to guide it into the child's face, but Aidan is not buying into the "Open the hangar wide for the airplane" bit. His jaws clamp shut like a bear trap.

Next come the threats: "You hurry up with that thing, or you know what's going to happen to you? We'll go shopping without you and leave you here." Aidan picks up his burger and holds it about two feet from his face as if there is at least a mathematical possibility that he might comply with the parental order.

Soon the corners of his mouth begin to tighten into a curt, self-satisfied smile. When Dad sees it, he jumps out of the booth and yells, "Okay, that's it! We're going shopping without you, and do you know what's going to happen to you, buddy? Cops are going to come get you!"

Aidan, no doubt, is thinking something like this: *Look at me. I'm only six years old, and I've totally controlled these two adults for twenty minutes without even opening my mouth. What a power trip! I control their tone of voice, the color of their faces, and whether or not they make fools of themselves in public. The last thing on my mind is worrying about being picked up by cops.*

Who's Controlling Whom?

Aidan's parents blew it entirely in trying to make him eat his food. Aidan had total control over what went down his food pipe. Had his parents offered him choices instead of making demands—had they taken only as much control as they absolutely needed—they would have been able to put Aidan in control on their terms. But how?

Two Ways to Leave with Me: Hungry or Not Hungry

Love and Logic parents would say, with a smile on their face, "No problem, Aidan. My car will be leaving in five minutes. There are two ways to leave with me: hungry is one way; not hungry is the other." That gives the parents as much control as they need. They don't need to control whether the burger goes down the child's throat—in fact, they *can't* control that. But the parents *can* control when the car leaves.

By offering Aidan the choices, the struggle is transferred inside Aidan's head. Aidan's too busy to argue—he's weighing his choices, *Hungry . . . not hungry . . . hungry . . . not hungry*—and Mom and Dad have five minutes of welcome tranquility. They gain control by relinquishing control. However, many parents, after issuing the alternatives, would be tempted to harp and nag while the child is making up his mind. They might say things like, "Don't forget, my car is leaving in three minutes. If you don't eat that food, you're going to be hungry. You'll wake up in the middle of the night, and there won't be anything to eat. It's going to be a miserable night." These sorts of reminders are put-downs. Cut the kid some slack. Aidan's smart enough to remember the choices he's been given.

Let Your Kids Know That Handling Them Is No Sweat for You

The old saying "Never let them see you sweat" applies here as well as in most Love and Logic encounters. Kids will take advantage of parents who give the impression that controlling them is difficult or that they have the power to aggravate their parents. Such frustration sends the covert message to the child that "I am difficult to handle. I must be a problem to my parents," whereas handling them easily with choices sends the message, "Dealing with me is no sweat for my parents—in fact, they seem to enjoy it! I must be a pretty good kid since I am no problem for them at all."

Human beings crave emotion. In fact, most folks believe God wants His people to love Him, so maybe even He craves emotion. People will pay big bucks to satisfy their cravings. Indeed, the most-requested speakers, the most sought-after entertainers, and the world's greatest sports stars are among the most highly paid people on earth. What do they have in common? They all stimulate our emotions.

There are a number of emotions effective in modifying behavior. Stark terror, for instance, brings quick response, but there's another common emotion almost as effective as stark terror. This emotion, generally given by adults to kids, affects children's behavior far more frequently than any other emotion. What is that emotion so frequently given to children?

You might guess love, but actually love is often very slow in motivating behavior. Not only that, it's often not effective. People who love each other often hurt each other the most. Love is important, for loving parents generally raise great kids. But to children, everyday, plain old love can be a little boring. It's not the movies about love that they love to see! Which movie do most kids want to see: *Jurassic Park* (about dinosaurs dining on humans) or a sweet little love story like *Sleepless in Seattle*? Most kids would rather see a dinosaur eat a lawyer in an outhouse any old day!

But by far the most effective emotion for modifying children's behavior is the showing of frustration. From a kid's point of view, frustration is an irresistible mix of wonderful emotions. Adult anger and adult loss of control—no kid could ask for anything more exciting! As a matter of fact, we all love frustration and loss of control by others. Most of today's sitcoms and many comic strips are based on frustrated authority figures.

The toddlerhood game of peekaboo and the subsequent, "Oh, no! You see me!" is often based on mock frustration. Kids love mock frustration. "Oh, no, you beat me to the car!" Whenever adults show real frustration, they give off vibrations of strong emotion, usually anger, and then delightfully declare they have no control in the situation. Frustration almost always indicates a loss of control. This is the irresistible combination frustration shows: The parent turns red, lights up, gets noisy, and hands control to the child. Now what kid wouldn't want that?!

Using the tools and techniques of Love and Logic when raising children is a parent's best insurance against feeling frustrated. Love and Logic parents may feel sad for their child, they may be empathetic about the consequences the child suffers, but Love and Logic parents are generally far too effective to be frustrated!

LOVE AND LOGIC TIP 20

"No Problem"

The phrase "No problem" is a lifesaver for the parent confronted with a misbehaving child. When Mom or Dad says it, even the dumbest kid in the world can figure out what it means: No problem for the adult, big problem for the kid. When we say, "No problem," we give ourselves a few precious seconds to come up with thinking words that will inform our children what we will do, not what they have to do.

Under Your Power or Under My Power

When Aidan's five minutes are up, Dad must then enforce this child's choice. He could use fighting words like, "You get in my car," but much better would be thinking words like, "My car is leaving now." Probably Aidan will say, "Yeah, but I'm not finished." Once again Dad would offer Aidan choices: "No problem, son. You can go under your own power or my power. Either one." The point Aidan must understand is that the car's leaving and Aidan's being in it doesn't depend on whether or not he's done eating. The car is leaving—period.

Assuming Aidan decides not to come with Dad willingly—a reasonable assumption, by the way—then Dad must pick Aidan up and head for the door with him. (An important note on choices: There are always three. In this example, Aidan can do it one way, or he can do it the other way. The third option is that the parent will decide. Aidan didn't decide, so his dad decided for him.)

A lot of parents are bothered by what comes next. After all, it is unlikely Aidan will look into Dad's eyes and coo, "Great parenting style, Dad." No, he will probably be kicking and screaming like a banshee. Everybody in Burger King will be watching every move Dad makes as he hauls this wild, flailing kid out the door. Let them watch. First, the people in the restaurant aren't saying to themselves, *Look what a bad parent that guy is.* They're thinking, *Thank goodness that's not* my *kid. Now I can eat in peace.* Second, parents of six-year-olds don't go into a place like Burger King to build lasting relationships with the other people dining there, so who cares what they think? And third, teaching a child responsibility is not a free ride.

We must steel ourselves for resistance and opposition. There's a price we must pay.

Keep the Parental Trap Buttoned

To ensure that Aidan has a learning experience from this incident, his mom and dad must remember one thing: to keep their mouths shut. Save the words for happy times. Again, Love and Logic parents have a limited vocabulary. The only time to reason with a child is when both parties are happy. Parents who enforce the consequences for their child with their mouths moving strip the consequences of their value. Allow the consequences to do the teaching.

Carrying the kicking and screaming Aidan out the restaurant door, Dad would then put him very gently in the car and drive off, all the while keeping mum about the incident. Before the evening is over, Aidan will probably say something very intelligent: "I'm hungry." When he says it, Dad should stifle the temptation to get angry and say, "Sure, you're hungry. I try to tell you these things, but you never listen. That'll teach you to eat your hamburger in the restaurant." Such a response only engenders more antagonism and resistance in the child.

Dad should administer the consequences with a compassionate sadness. For example: "Oh, for sure, son. That's what happens to me when I miss my dinner. I'll bet you'll be anxious for breakfast. Don't worry—we'll cook a good one." Without doubt, Aidan will learn more from this response than from anger and threats. Sorrow and consequences and an arm around his shoulder are powerful teaching agents.

LOVE AND LOGIC TIP 21

The Brain Drain

Children are going to fight the choices we give them. Rare are the kids who will always choose one of the given choices and happily go on with life. Sometimes they'll fight with a vengeance.

One of children's favorite ploys is "Brain Drain." In "Brain Drain," they attempt to make us do the thinking, thus draining our brains of energy. Guilt, indecision, telling us we don't love them—they'll lay anything on us that comes to mind with words such as, "That's not fair," and "You don't love me." Every time they do this, we are forced to drain our energy tank in supplying justification for the choices we give them. However, if anyone is going to drain anyone's brain, let it be us draining our children's brain. We do this by holding firm to our choices. Observe the following scenario:

NICK: "Hey, Dad, bye. I'll see ya. I'm going outside with Mason."
DAD: "Hold on, Nick, I think you promised you'd have the garage swept by this morning before you did anything else."
NICK: "But I don't have time right now, Dad."
DAD: "That may be so, son, and feel free to go as soon as you sweep the garage."
NICK: "Aw, c'mon. I promised my friends I'd go."
DAD: "I'm sure that's true, Nick, and feel free to go as soon as you sweep the garage."
NICK: "I'll do it when I get back. Mason does his chores after he plays."
DAD: "I'm sure that's true, Nick, and feel free to go as soon as you sweep the garage."

Repeat the choices over and over again. Don't get angry. Stick to your guns, and your brain will remain refreshingly full. Most kids will get frustrated with this after three or four tries, thinking, *How quickly can I get out of this crazy situation?* Out loud they will say, "I know. Don't say it again."

Choose Your Choices Carefully

Many well-meaning parents who offer choices to their children err in their delivery of those choices. Often they offer their children two choices—one the adults can live with, and one the adults cannot live with. For example, back in our Burger King example, had Aidan's dad said, "You either eat that or you stay here," Aidan probably would have decided to hang around until the place closed for the evening. Kids have a way of finding the jugular in any conflict.

Be mindful that it is easy to turn the choices into threats that tell the youngster, "Choose my way or else." When we say to our child, "You can either clean your room or lose your right to watch television," it is no different from our boss saying to us, "Would you rather do that report today or get fired?" We must offer real choices, not threats:

- "Would you rather clean your room this morning or this afternoon?" (If the child says, "Neither," wise parents say, "Not a wise decision. I'll get back to you on this." Consequences need not be immediate.)

- "Would you rather pick up your toys or hire me to do it?"
- "Do you want to spend your allowance on fun things this week or pay someone to do your chores?"
- "Do you guys want to settle the problem yourselves or draw straws to see who sits by the car window?"

Nonthreatening choices, offered in a calm manner, give children a chance to take some control over their problems.

Rules for Giving Choices

In summary, as we offer choices to our kids, we should remember five basic points:

1. Always be sure to select choices that you as a parent like and can live with. Don't provide one you like and one you don't, because the child will usually select the one you don't like.
2. Never give a choice unless you are willing to allow the child to experience the consequences of that choice.
3. Never give choices when the child is in danger.
4. Always give only two verbal choices, but make sure the child knows there is an implied third choice: If he doesn't decide, then you'll decide for him.
5. Your delivery is important. Try to start your sentence with one of the following:

    - "You're welcome to____or ____."
    - "Feel free to___or_____."
    - "Would you rather_____or_____ ?"
    - "What would be best for you— ______ or_____ ?"

7

The Recipe for Success: Empathy with Consequences

My child, if your heart is wise,
my heart too will be glad.
Proverbs 23:15

When Jim's kids were young, he had a problem with them going to bed on time. If he had a dollar for every time he shouted at his kids, "You guys get in that bed right now and go to sleep!" he'd be relaxing at his summer home in the Bahamas. As a concerned parent, he knew that lack of sleep would make the next day miserable for his kids. They'd drag around, unable to think clearly or perform well at school. Why, they might even fall asleep at their desks! That seemed too high a price for his kids to pay, so he kept badgering them to go to sleep on time and threatening to spank them, take away television privileges, or take them out of sports.

One day a great truth of parenting was revealed to him: You can't *make* a child go to sleep. So he marched upstairs, called his kids together, and said, "Kids, I've got to apologize. I've been meddling in your life. I've been trying to tell you things you should be deciding on your own. So if you can remember two simple little rules, I'll never hassle you again about going to sleep. Think you can handle that?"

"Yeah," they said, "we can handle that."

"Rule one," Jim said, "is that from eight o'clock on is private time for your mom and me. We don't want to see or hear you, but feel free to be awake. Rule two: We all get up at six o'clock every morning. See you at six o'clock." He gave them each a little kiss and went back to the family room.

At 10:30 p.m., the lights in both Jim's kids' rooms were still on. Attempting to provide them with an admirable model to emulate, he wandered into their rooms and said, "Well, I'm going to bed. I don't want to be grouchy in the morning. See you then."

When he got up at six the next morning, the lights were still blazing away. One child was sleeping with his clothes on; another had come to rest in a sitting position in the corner. He then discovered another great truth of parenting: It's a lot easier to wake kids up than to put them to sleep. Turning two radios up to front-row-rock-concert decibel level takes hardly any energy at all.

Three bleary-eyed and moaning kids wandered around the house that morning, rubbing their eyes and whining, "I'm too tired to go to school today," "I'm sick, Dad," and "I want to go back to bed."

Jim didn't get angry with them. Instead, he felt genuine sadness for their plight. "Well, for sure, kids," he said, "that's what happens to me, too, when I stay up too late. I bet it's going to be a long day at school. Well, try to have as good a day as you possibly can, under the circumstances. We'll see you when you get home. Have a nice day."

He watched them make their way to the bus stop. At 3:30 p.m., the bus pulled up on the return trip, and from its door staggered six-year-old Charlie, who wearily traipsed up the stairs and found his bed. There he slept the rest of the afternoon with his baseball hat crunched down over his nose, his heavy jacket still on, and his tundra boots laced up to his knees.

At dinner that night, Charlie kept nodding off. However, before the meal was over, he said a most intelligent thing: "I think I'll go to bed early."

It took Charlie one night to learn a lesson Jim had spent years trying to teach him. And it happened because Jim was empathetic and allowed the consequences to do the teaching.

Had Jim paddled his kids or taken away television privileges, he wouldn't have been nearly as effective in teaching his kids the lesson about the importance of a good night's sleep. He would have been using punishment, and the real world by and large doesn't operate on punishment.

Hurting from the Inside Out

As we give our kids control, we remember that control can corrupt, and absolute control can corrupt absolutely. Learning how to handle power and control is essential if our children are to grow to be good leaders. As children misuse their power and control, unwise parents show frustration, anger, and often plead. Wise parents allow natural and imposed consequences to do the teaching. And they are empathetic. When Abe, a star basketball player, used his power and influence incorrectly and was barred from playing in three important games, his dad was secretly very pleased. But what he said to Abe was, "I know that the coach's call makes you very unhappy, but I'm sure you can handle it. At this point, do you blame the coach entirely, or do you think there may have been things you could have handled differently?" So control and power are handled like money. We rejoice when the child handles them correctly, and we show empathy without rescue when unwise choices result in consternation, pain, and regret.

Imagine yourself banging a fender in the parking lot at work. You feel bad about it, and when you come home that evening, you explain the accident to your spouse. "What!" your loving mate shrieks. "That really makes me mad. You know how you wanted to go skiing this weekend? Well, forget it. You're grounded!"

A ridiculous scenario? Of course. As adults we don't get grounded when we mess up in life; nobody washes our mouths out with soap when we swear. Punishments don't happen in the real world unless crimes are committed. When people are punished for something, they seldom pause for self-examination. Resentment is the more common reaction.

The same holds true for children. When we send kids to bed early because they sassed us, we are doling out punishment. When children tote home all Ds and Fs on a report card and we rescind television privileges for two months, we are not allowing the consequences of mistakes to do the teaching.

LOVE AND LOGIC TIP 22

Warning: Good Parents Don't Give Warnings

Imagine that you're heading down the freeway doing 85 in a 70-mph zone. You see the multicolored lights of doom blinking in your rearview mirror, and you think of one thing, and one thing only: "I'm going to get a ticket." The cop saunters up to your car, nice as can be, writes the ticket, bids you adieu, and is on his merry way. He offers no hysterics, no anger, no threats. Just courtesy and a little slip of paper—the consequences of your breaking the law.

As an adult, you would never think, in your wildest imaginings, of telling him, "I'll be good, officer. Honest, I won't speed anymore," and having him say, "Well, okay. If you'll be good, I won't write you a ticket." That is the stuff of fantasy. But how often in our homes is our kids' pleading met with parental shilly-shallying?

Little Adam is a terror at the table. He pouts and complains and whines and builds miniature motocross courses on his plate on which he pushes peas up and down ramps of celery stalks and mini-mountains of mashed potatoes.

Mom, thinking she's consequential, says, "Okay, Adam, your dinner's over. Off to your room."

Adam says, "I'll be good."

And what does Mom say but, "Oh, well, okay. Are you sure you'll be good? Or are you going to keep goofing off at the table?"

"No, I won't do it anymore. I'll be good."

"Well, okay," Mom says, thinking her problems are over. "You can stay."

The real world doesn't operate on the multiple-warning system, and neither should we. Parents who give a lot of warnings raise kids who don't behave until they've had a lot of warnings.

The real world operates on consequences. If we do a consistently lousy job at work, our boss doesn't take away our VCR—he fires us.

When we punish our children, we provide them with a great escape valve, an escape from the consequences of their action. They never have to think when they're punished. They don't have to change their behavior. They think, *I'm being punished for what I did. I'm doing my time.* And their anger is directed toward the punisher: us.

As Love and Logic parents, we want our kids to hurt from the inside out. This happens when we allow the consequences to do the teaching. Consequences leave kids thinking very hard about their behavior and their responsibilities. Consequences lead to self-examination and thought.

Naturally Occurring Consequences

The best consequences are those that fall naturally. If Aubrey is a nuisance at the dinner table and chooses to play on the floor rather than eat nicely at the table, then it only makes sense that she'll be hungry at bedtime. If Seth continually neglects his schoolwork and brings home failing grades, then staying back a grade makes sense. Naturally falling consequences allow the cause and effect of our children's actions to register in their brains. When they ask themselves, *Who is making me hurt like this?* their only answer is, *Me.*

But these consequences put a painful, sinking feeling into our stomachs as parents. They're exactly the things we don't want to happen to our children. Dylan gets cold when he doesn't wear his jacket. Samantha gets hungry when she goes to bed without eating. We are tempted to remind them of the pain of cold and the misery of hunger. But if we want the consequences to do their work effectively, we cannot afford to take that luxury.

Cole, age nine, was a sleepyhead. Every morning, he'd beat to death the snooze alarm on his bedside clock. Seven o'clock, then 7:10, then 7:20, and every time the jarring buzz of his alarm rattled his ears, his fist would promptly pound on the snooze button, and he'd be back in dreamland.

Mom quickly tired of this every-morning hassle, and she decided to let the consequences teach her son a lesson. One day when Cole roared downstairs twenty minutes before school was to start, warmly yet firmly she said, "Oh, glad to see you're up. What do you think you'll do today in your room?"

"In my room?" Cole said. "I'm going to school!"

"Well, that's good," Mom said. "How are you going to get there? The bus left ten minutes ago."

"You're going to take me, of course," Cole replied.

"Oh, sorry," Mom said. "I can't do that. I'll be busy with my housework all day. Feel free to arrange other transportation or spend the rest of the day in your room so I can do my work without any interruptions, just like on other school days.

"When lunchtime comes, feel free to make something for yourself," Mom continued. "And if I go on any errands this afternoon, I'll take care of getting a babysitter for you. But don't worry if you can't pay the sitter. You can pay me back later in the week, or I can take it out of your allowance. But you have to worry about that only if I have to go out on an errand. So it's not a problem right now. Have a nice day, Cole. I'll see you at 3:30 when you normally get home on the bus."

Of course, when the next morning rolled around, Cole wanted an excuse note. Mom said, "Oh, I can understand that. I know how nice a note is to explain why you were absent from school. But you know I only write notes for you when you're sick. Hope it works out okay with your teacher though. Have a nice day, under the circumstances."

There's no question—doing this takes guts! But the reward of changed behavior is worth it. These consequences all fall naturally and fit the "crime" of not getting up in time for school. Cole misses school, he's out of his mom's hair just like any other school day, and he doesn't get a note.

Amazingly, kids never seem to miss more than two days of school in a row with this technique. Without the company of others and without the attention of a parent who nags them, they become conspicuously unhappy.

LOVE AND LOGIC TIP 23

A Real-World Bus Service

When Jordan, age twelve, first came into our (Foster's) home as a foster son, we knew he was passive-resistant and would have trouble being on time. His "thing" was being late. Therefore, during his first week with us, we arranged a learning experience for him.

Jordan wanted to be dropped off in town and meet us at a grocery store about ten miles from our mountain home. I told Jordan I would be glad to drop him off in town and that I could meet him at the grocery store at 5:00 p.m. Then I added, "Jordan, I operate like the bus service does in the real world. However, I'm a little bit more lenient. I will wait three minutes. If you are at the grocery store between 5:00 and 5:03, I'll pick you up. If, for some reason, you can't make that time, don't worry. I'll swing back past and wait from 10:00 to 10:03. If, due to poor planning, you can't make it then, don't worry. I'll swing by at seven tomorrow morning on my way to work. I'll wait from 7:00 to 7:03."

Well, I knew Jordan would test me, and he did. When I went at 5:00, no Jordan. When I went at 10:00, I waited three minutes and then started to drive away. As I was pulling off, out of the shadows ran Jordan. He was waving his arms wildly over his head shouting in the night, "Here I am, here I am! Don't leave me!" I think that little episode had a definite beneficial effect, and although Jordan had been chronically late for his parents, he never was late for us.

Imposing Consequences

While naturally occurring consequences are best, occasionally our children's actions don't lend themselves to such consequences. In those cases, we must impose the consequences ourselves.

The art of arranging consequences comes naturally to some parents, while others must gain this type of expertise through practice. Often parents choose to impose consequences that are irrelevant or, if relevant, the consequences are either too harsh or too lenient.

When no consequences occur naturally, the imposed consequences must (1) be enforceable, (2) fit the "crime," and (3) be laid down firmly in love. Sometimes these imposed consequences look conspicuously like punishments. But when imposed without anger and threats, and when presented to our children in a way that the connection between their misbehavior and the consequences is made plain, they are quite effective.

LOVE AND LOGIC TIP 24

Empathy, Not Anger

Letting the consequences do the teaching isn't enough. We as parents must show our empathy—our sincere, loving concern—when the consequences hit. That's what drives the lesson home with our children without making them feel as though we're not "on their side." Consider the following examples:

Aaron misses dinner because he didn't do his chores on time.

ANGRY WORDS: "Of course you're hungry! I bet you won't do that again. I told you you'd be hungry."

EMPATHETIC WORDS: "I know how that feels, son. I'm hungry, too, when I miss a meal, but we'll have a big breakfast."

Lindsay is tired in the morning because she stayed up too late.

ANGRY WORDS: "I told you you'd be tired if you didn't go to bed on time. Now you're going to suffer all day at school."

EMPATHETIC WORDS: "Oh, you're tired, huh? I feel the same way at work when I don't get my sleep. But have the best day you can, under the circumstances."

Colton gets low grades on his report card.

ANGRY WORDS: "You don't do your homework, and now you come home with lousy grades. That ought to teach you a lesson."

EMPATHETIC WORDS: "Oh, how awful. During my school years, I got some poor grades when I didn't apply myself, but there's always next semester."

Consequences Don't Have to Be Immediate

Consequences don't have to be doled out on the spot to be effective. In fact, they are often most effective after a child thinks they have gotten away with inappropriate behavior.

Two grade-schoolers, Colette and Mia, are riding to the shopping center in the backseat of the family car. After they bicker, punch, and push, their mom draws the obligatory imaginary line down the middle of the backseat to keep them out of each other's hair. Then come the screams from one or the other: "Mom, Colette's on my side!" or "Mom, Mia punched me!"

Mom has had enough of it. The next time they were about to go shopping, Mom said, "The last time we went to the shopping center, there was a lot of fighting in the backseat. It invaded my ears and made it so I couldn't concentrate on the road. I've decided to take a quiet drive to the stores today. I've arranged for a babysitter to stay with you. But don't worry about paying her right this minute. You can pay me on Saturday or we can take it out of your allowance. But you don't need to decide about that right away. You can tell me later how you want to handle that."

Had Mom blown up on the spot at the kids in the backseat, nothing would have been learned nor would the girls have had much time to think about their actions. However, by letting some time pass, the kids have probably let the incident slip from their minds. But as they now sit home with the babysitter, they have several things to think about: *How are we going to pay for this? How are we going to get Mom to take us with her next time? How am I going to get along with my sister?* and so on. Not only that, but this imposed consequence is enforceable.

When Hunter comes home late from playing at a neighbor boy's house, a suitable consequence would be imposed the next time he asks to go to the neighbor boy's house. His mother could say, "Remember how you were late coming home last time? I'm not up to worrying about that today, so you may stay home this time and play by yourself or watch television. We'll talk about it again the next time you want to go over there." The consequence is thus tied in Hunter's mind to returning on time from the neighbor boy's house.

Good consequences don't always pop right into our brains. Even professionals in the field can't always think up immediate consequences. This is another reason why delaying consequences is often the best thing to do. It allows us time to consider the best actions as well as get ideas from others.

If no consequence comes to mind, it is much better to take our time and think of an appropriate consequence than to blurt something out in haste or anger. We are no less effective as parents when we take a little time to think through consequences. Much-needed time for thinking can be bought with the following words:

- "I'm not sure what to do about this right now, but I'll let you know."
- "You know, I've never been the parent of a five-year-old boy before, so I'll have to give this some thought. I'll get back to you on it."
- "I'm not sure how to react to that. I'll have to give it some thought."

Then, if you really want to drive the point home, you can add, "Try not to worry about it." Chances are that doing so will ensure that your kids do nothing *but* consider their actions over the next few days.

Giving ourselves time to consider consequences helps our kids too. They have time to agonize over the possible consequences, and that is quality thinking time.

LOVE AND LOGIC TIP 25

Consequences with Humor

Love and Logic emphasizes consequences, and consequences can sometimes be painful. But let us never forget that Love and Logic puts the pizzazz, zip, and fun into parenting and leadership in general. People use Love and Logic because it makes them feel good. Just like "a spoonful of sugar helps the medicine go down," creativity and a sense of humor can also help the consequences go down.

This leads me (Foster) to share a wonderful story with you that was recently told to me after a workshop. I can take no credit for it, and if I could credit the wonderful mom who told it to me, of course I would.

My husband was the quiet—and sometimes drill sergeant—type, and as we viewed your videotapes, he would sometimes laugh and comment. Yet

> I never knew if the Love and Logic principles were sinking in with him until one day, in the car, when we were driving together and the kids were raising low-grade heck and high water in the backseat, he said, just as you have said on a tape, "Guys, it's going to be a lot quieter in this car the last mile home because your mom and I will be the only ones in here!"
>
> There was a moment of deafening silence, and then our ten-year-old son, in a slightly challenging and snarky voice, said, "You wouldn't do that!"
>
> Quick as a wink, my hubby said, "That's what Tommy said."
>
> Again a moment of silence. Then one of the kids asked, "Who's Tommy?"
>
> My husband replied, "Your older brother!"
>
> A mile from home, the kids got out and hiked home, and, of course, we never had to use that method again. But the cute and wonderful thing is now that the kids are grown and travel with their families on trips, they write us and sign it, "Poor lost Tommy." It's the family joke. Wandering Tom is still out there somewhere, wandering the highways and byways of the world after being kicked out of the car and becoming lost on the way home.
>
> I think the lessons in this woman's story are clear. When the going gets tough, the tough start laughing—laughing, joking, and loving kids while imposing the consequences sets the model for their own development of great coping skills.

It's the Empathy That Counts

You have probably noticed that Love and Logic parents react quite differently from other parents when kids make mistakes. We don't get angry, we don't say, "I told you so," and we don't sit our kids down and lecture them about their errors. If we did those things, we would be impeding the logic of the consequences from doing their thing. The child's anger would be directed toward us and not toward the lesson the consequences teach. Also, when we sit kids down and explain to them—even in the nicest terms—what they did wrong and why it didn't work out, we deflect their thinking from their own consequences to us. We only hinder the power of the consequences when we do that.

The thing that drives the lesson into our children's hearts after they make a mistake is our empathy and sadness. We put the relationship between us and our children foremost in our minds. Our love for them reigns supreme. We have been building their self-esteem from infancy, telling them they are loved, skillful, and capable. And a foul-up, regardless of how serious on their part, doesn't change anything. They must be told that message continually.

So when our children make a mistake, we really ache for them—we know what it's like. And we tell them this in all seriousness. When our kids blow it and suffer the consequences, it is crucial that we express our sadness to them.

LOVE AND LOGIC TIP 26

Messages That Lock In Empathy

When our kids mess up, we are often overcome with anger and want to punish them. The better thing to do, though, is lock in our empathy for them and then let the consequences do the teaching. Parents should let their kids know how much they love them and how badly they feel about their decision and their problem as the result of it as soon as it happens. Before getting angry or sucked into the child's problem, try using one of the following statements:

- "What a bummer."
- "Really? I know you, and I'm sure you'll come up with something."
- "That's terrible. How are you going to handle it?"
- "Oh, no, I'm glad that's not my paper (report card, grade, late assignment, specific problem). You must feel awful. What can you do?"
- "Hmmm, that's really an interesting way of looking at it. Let me know how that turns out."
- "Wow, what a mess. Let me know what you come up with."

When we make these types of comments we don't put ourselves up against our kids; we put ourselves squarely on their side, and on the side of their learning from their mistakes. They need to know we will be with them through it all but that we will not take away any of their responsibility in the process.

Michelle was well on her way to becoming a Love and Logic parent. She strove to give away the control she didn't need, and she always made sure Brianne, her sixth-grade daughter, had to do more thinking than she did.

When Brianne came home from school one day with a D on her spelling test, Michelle's parenting philosophy was put to a more rigorous test. Michelle kept hearing a voice in her head that said, "This could be a great opportunity. Don't blow it by reminding her." And Michelle didn't reprimand her daughter. She also knew that the teacher had provided the consequence, so she didn't say anything about that either.

Michelle did exactly what she knew was right. She felt sorry for her daughter. She balanced the consequences with an equal amount of empathy. She said, "Oh, it must really be embarrassing to get a D. I bet it's hard to face your teacher when you haven't done your studying. I bet you feel awful."

Brianne got very quiet and was thinking about what she had done. Then Michelle thought of a Love and Logic principle: *When you run out of things to say, transfer the problem to the youngster by asking a question.* So Michelle said, "What are you going to do, Brianne?"

Brianne, with a downcast face, meekly replied, "I don't know what I'm going to do."

So far so good. Michelle had the control she needed, and Brianne, with all her thinking, was owning the problem and devising solutions. But then Michelle slipped up and said, "Because you refuse to study, you're not going to the party on Friday."

"What do you mean I'm not going to the party?" Brianne yelled. "It's not my fault I got a D! You should see the words that teacher gives. She never gives us time to study, and she never helps me when I raise my hand. It's just not fair!"

Allowing consequences while showing empathy is one of the toughest parts of Love and Logic parenting. Anger is such an appealing emotion, especially when we use it on our children. Punishment makes us feel so powerful. It makes us think we're in control. Anger and punishment, put in concert with each other, provide a deadly duo of counterproductive parenting.

The entire lesson Brianne was learning was demolished by Michelle's punishment. For the consequences to have any benefit, we must commiserate *with* our kids, not yell *at* them. They have nobody to be angry with but themselves when we show sadness. Because of punishment, Brianne had her mom to blame.

We are constantly giving messages to our kids, but the overriding message of all must be one telling them they're okay. They may be having a hard time with their lives, they may have made a mistake and will have to live with the consequences, but we're in their corner and love them just the same. Empathy about the consequences shows our kids that kind of love. It allows the logic of the consequences to do the teaching.

8

Lights, Camera, Parenting!

I have taught you the way of wisdom;
I have led you in the paths
of uprightness.
When you walk, your step will
not be hampered;
and if you run, you will not stumble.
Proverbs 4:11-12

A fifty-year-old man approached a musician and asked, "Can you teach me to play the trombone so I can play in the town civic band and in parades and other things?"

"Sure," the musician said.

"How long will it take?" the aspiring trombonist asked.

"Well," the musician said, "I could teach almost anybody to play anything he wanted to play in five years' time."

"Five years!" the would-be student said. "I'll be fifty-five years old by then!"

"Yes, you will," the musician returned. "And how old will you be in five years if you don't learn how to play the trombone?"

Practice, Practice, Practice

Love and Logic ideas may seem overwhelming. There's much to remember: thinking words, separation of problems, choices, empathy with the consequences. It's enough to exasperate anyone unschooled in the Love and Logic style—that is, were they to try to apply it all at once.

However, Love and Logic parenting is like dieting. Dieters do not say, "I'm going to become thin today," and, presto, become thin. Likewise, parents don't say, "These kids of mine are going to shape up for good right now." So if Love and Logic is brand-new to you, implement it a little at a time. Pick one thing that bothers you about your child's behavior—one thing that you think you would have good success of correcting with Love and Logic principles—and then work on it with one principle you have learned from this book. But don't do it right away. Rehearse it first. Figure out how your child might react, and prepare yourself to deal with that reaction. Once you've succeeded in one small area, pick another area and work on it, then another, and so on.

The following five-point guideline will help you mentally rehearse Love and Logic:

1. Pick the situation and what you want the child to do.
2. Picture yourself standing tall, looking directly into your child's eyes and having a perfect right to expect what you are about to request. Check yourself in a mirror.
3. Imagine the sound of your voice.
4. Try it out on friends and get their opinions.
5. Rehearse this until you hear yourself saying, "Kid, make my day. Let me strut my new stuff!"

The time to actually implement the strategy is when you have the time, the energy, and enough backup support for your actions. Kids will test you, they will get angry, they will try anything to make you revert to your old ways—even to the point of saying, "Mom, I liked you better before you read that dumb parenting book!" Once you encounter resistance, you'll know it's working. But hold firm. If they can control you by pushing your anger, sympathy, or guilt button, they'll come rushing back to it whenever they feel the need for control.

As you implement Love and Logic parenting, you will find that you will grow as much as your children do. With every success you experience, your self-concept will develop as much as theirs does.

What Love and Logic Is Not

Over the years since we started the research that led to this book and through the seminars and research that have followed, we discovered how good ideas and practices can be misconstrued, misrepresented, and taken out of context. So it's been said that "the road to hell is paved with good intentions." Perhaps on the way down, one might meet teens raised by parents who read books on how to raise little angels. What went wrong?

Love and Logic does not guarantee angelic children and teens, but we do know that the concepts, tools, and techniques of Love and Logic provide the best chance for parental success. But even Love and Logic can be misconstrued or misused. Love and Logic material is filled with beautiful constructs that can be misapplied even by well-meaning parents, especially if their own background is one of dysfunction, abuse, and pain.

One of the interesting things about the Love and Logic method is that if you don't do it exactly right, it simply won't work. For instance, we place a great deal of emphasis on modeling. This is one of the great "E's" of Love and Logic—*example*—which, along with *experience* and *empathy*, we feel forms the great backbone of effective parenting. And we attempt throughout this book to help parents understand how to set healthy, win-win examples. When parents have poor self-image, it's hard to set the example that even they themselves want their children to emulate.

Since writing the first edition of this book, we have discovered some common confusions unique to Love and Logic newbies. Specific Love and Logic attitudes, tools, and techniques can be misapplied or misunderstood. We would like to help you avoid some of these pitfalls by exploring a few of these sad, if understandable, areas of confusion. Perhaps this is a little self-serving, for we have been shocked over the years, watching or hearing of parents doing the darnedest things, but were doubly shocked to learn they would often defend their actions by saying proudly, "I learned this from Love and Logic." Here are a few of the more common ones we have encountered in the years since the first printing of this book.

Using insincere empathy.
Love and Logic emphasizes leading with empathy, such as saying:

- "How sad."
- "What a bummer."
- "Hope things go better for you."
- "If anyone can learn from this mistake, it's you."
- "I'm sure it's hard to be you at times."
- "If anyone can cope with this, it's you."
- "When the going gets tough, the tough get going."
- "That's a problem for you, that's for sure."
- "With a little deeper figuring, you'll probably come up with good answers."

All of these statements—meant to be expressed with kindness, empathy, and understanding—can, unfortunately, also be uttered with the warmth of an icicle on a frosty morning. Unbelievable, but true! This is why. Some parents, understandably, in attempting to learn to show empathy, are on unfamiliar ground. They are used to being angry and frustrated. So, while trying to remember to use new statements—feeling unsure of themselves and perhaps insecure with a new knowledge that doesn't "feel" familiar—they make statements with the right words but wrong meaning. Their old disappointment leaks through with unhappy, angry, critical, or sarcastic demeanor.

True empathetic statements are not generated from the head but from the heart! Every so often we have heard parents say, "Bummer for you," with such callousness that it would freeze a river in summer. For example, Robert failed a test due to not studying. His mom, just learning the Love and Logic principle of not owning or solving another's problem, says, "Too bad for you that you didn't put more effort into studying for that test," and experiences a wisp of cold from her son that cuts her heart like the breeze off ice in winter. Another mom, following the same reasoning, puts her arm around her son's shoulder and says, "Honey, it's hard to study when it seems that other things are more important, isn't it?" and the sun seems to come out from behind the clouds to melt the frost on the windows.

The delivery, and the heart behind it, can make all the difference in the world.

Using consequences as threats rather than a logical outcome of their actions.

Sometimes when a consequence is uttered as a threat, it's pretty obvious: "Gavin, if you can't sit still, I am going to send you to your room!" Perhaps the threat is still obvious when a parent says, "If you don't know how to behave properly, I don't want you around me at all."

It's a happier child and parent when the adults impose consequences to take care of themselves. The child is still offered choices: "Ethan, when you act like that it really hurts my eyes and my ears. Where else would you feel comfortable doing that?"

Giving choices that do not give reasonable or acceptable alternatives.

Some choices just aren't good, honest, and true choices. Spencer was giving Lauren a really hard time in the backseat, when their mom, having had it with Spencer, from behind the steering wheel said, "Spencer, when I pull over, do you want me to allow Lauren to hit you, or do you want me to smack you myself?"

Love and Logic parents give their children choices within acceptable limits that follow a few key guidelines:

1. The child is expected to willingly pick one of the choices, not given two choices that are both unappealing.
2. The parent can live with whatever choice is picked.
3. If the choice is refused, the parent can lovingly take his or her turn at choosing a response that is enforceable. (Don't rush into this. Enforceable responses sometimes take thought: "Hmmm . . . That response drains my energy. I'll get back to you on this.")

Using "taking care of yourself" as an excuse for selfishness.

Selfishness; selflessness; self-centered; centered with self. These can be confusing terms with many nuances. And when parents come from difficult backgrounds, the important differences can be lost. For instance, it's considered good to be *selfless*, but to have *no sense of self* is bad. It's good to be *centered in yourself*, but to be *self-centered* is bad.

The reason this issue is important is because Love and Logic stresses the importance of parents taking good care of themselves to set the model for their children. If parents take good care of themselves, then children have a good chance of growing up to be adults who take good care of themselves. When parents always put the children first, they risk putting themselves last and raising entitled, demanding children (better known as spoiled brats).

Love and Logic parents need to put themselves first in a "centered in self" way that is not selfish but insists on a win-win relationship. Toddlers don't naturally put their parents first—they're not supposed to. So parents must teach children, in the second year of life, "I love you so much. First I win, and then look how well it works out for you! When I'm happy, you are happy too."

During adolescence, children who haven't learned the win-win message at two or thereafter often carefully manipulate rebellious win-lose situations with their parents. These generally deteriorate into lose-lose propositions that are upsetting for everyone. Therefore, when living with adolescents, Love and Logic parents insist on respect. They take good care of themselves, even if it means that their demanding and rebellious offspring may suffer unhappy consequences in the short run.

Using Love and Logic statements as a means of manipulation. As the old saying goes, "Kids don't care how much you know until they know how much you care." We provide Love and Logic techniques so that you can win the key power struggles you need to with your kids so that they learn to be responsible, not so that you can control every aspect of their lives. In fact, Love and Logic, in truth, is more about gradually giving up control to your kids over the years, not gaining more. Kids need to know you are doing this because you love them and want them to grow into great adults, not because you are constantly on some power or control trip.

Using Love and Logic techniques in lieu of building relationships with your children.
As we started researching Love and Logic, we took it for granted that all parents love their children and want the best for them. We still believe this is true, even though for some parents this is more difficult to express than it is for others. Some who must juggle an incredible number of plates have trouble with this because they just don't have the time. Still others never had good models for building relationships in the past and aren't sure where to begin with their own kids, so rather than confront the issue, they flee into hobbies, television, or other forms of avoiding their children.

One of the primary benefits of using Love and Logic is that it eliminates many of the factors that traditionally divide children from their parents—namely, anger, lectures, threats, and warnings. Love and Logic tools are usable, easy, and fun to use. So it is easy to overuse them. For instance, it is possible to use the "Uh-Oh" song with a toddler who is just being age appropriate. Perhaps not a bundle of joy, but not needing to be excused to his or her room, either. Overuse or misuse of fun-to-use tools is understandable but not excusable.

For example, a commonly used tool is the "I love you too much to argue" statement. Foster talked with a Montana mother, and she told him about a neat little kid who seemed to be more negative and angry after she frequently used, and turns out overused, "I love you too much to argue." Foster asked her what her son was most upset about. She responded that he frequently said, "Mom, you just don't listen to me." After exploring the situation, Mom realized that she was using "I love you too much to argue" instead of giving caring responses. She was repeating "I love you too much to argue" instead of simply getting down on one knee and saying, with love, "Honey, I'll discuss this later. I'm in a hurry right now. Thanks." More importantly, she realized she really was using the phrase as a way of short-circuiting listening.

Love and Logic cannot change the child before it changes the parent.
One of the reasons we emphasize over and over again that parents need to take care of themselves first is that if the adults are stressed, on edge, angry, or simply not taking care of themselves in a healthy way, Love and Logic will not work for them. Unless parents who have continually

dealt with their kids in anger in the past deal with defusing that anger first, they are still likely to fall back into that pattern every time they consequence their kids.

In Love and Logic, parents lead. If we want our kids to have self-control, then we must model it in front of them. If we want our kids to be responsible, then we must model that responsibility in dealing with them. If we want our kids to treat us and speak to us with respect, in addition to demanding it by our actions, we must treat and speak to them with respect. That is the parenting with Love and Logic two-step—first the parent, then the child.

It's Never Too Late to Start

Even if our kids are in their teens and have never been exposed to Love and Logic discipline, they—and we—can benefit from our putting it to use. The important thing is to build a relationship with our kids that will last a lifetime—long past the end of their adolescent years. And it is never too late to work on that.

Our children are our most precious resource. They come to us with one request: "During our short eighteen years with you, please teach us the truth about life and prepare us to be responsible adults when we leave home and enter the real world." In the course of those eighteen years, we'll be faced with many challenges in parenting our kids. Our love will be on the line every time they have a problem. That love has the potential to be either ally or enemy—to either help our children learn what they need to know, or to prevent them from growing to be responsible adults.

Let's grant our kids' request. Let's love them enough to allow them to learn the necessary and crucial skills of responsible thinking and living.

Part 2

Love and Logic Parenting Tools

How to Use Love and Logic Pearls

Knowing some basic concepts on parenting is a good beginning; they offer a foundation on which to build a system of discipline. But putting those ideas into practical use puts us on more treacherous ground. How do we handle children who pull a volcanic eruption whenever they don't win a struggle of wills? What about those little guys who meet even our kindest inquiry with the words "Get out of my face, sucker"? How about the children who won't go to bed on time, get up, do chores, do homework, or feed the pets? We don't want philosophy—we want answers! How do thinking words, choices, and empathy with the consequences play themselves out in real, practical, get-down parenting?

The second half of this book consists of forty-eight Love and Logic pearls, each one addressing one of the most common disciplinary problems a parent will meet during a child's first twelve years. In these pearls, we have explored and discussed individual challenges and given sound, practical advice on how to deal with them. Many of the pearls also contain a sample dialogue that shows how to discuss the issue with the child.

But reader beware: Do not try these pearls until you've read the first half of the book. Don't try to build the house until you've laid the foundation.

Pearl 1

Allowances/Money

There comes a time in the life of every child when financial responsibility pokes its foreboding snout through the tent flap of his or her world. We call it an allowance. It usually begins when a child is five or six years old.

We give children allowances because we want to teach them money management. Kids who have to struggle with money become not only more fiscally responsible but also more responsible in all areas of life.

Several helpful rules on allowances will help our kids make the most of this terrific learning experience:

> ***Rule One: Children do not earn their allowances.*** That means we do not pay them to do their chores. Being paid for chores robs them of the dignity of holding up their fair share of the family workload. The only time we'd pay them for chores is when they do *our* chores.
>
> ***Rule Two: Provide the allowance at the same time every week.*** This can be done with pay envelopes. Place the cash, plus a small invoice indicating the breakdown of the funds (for example, for a child in first grade, "$1 allowance, $6 lunch money") inside an envelope with the child's name on it. Sign the invoice, "Because we love you. Spend it wisely and make it last." The child must then tend to the envelope.
>
> ***Rule Three: Never insist that children save the allowance.*** They can't learn to handle money if they stash their allowance

in a shoe box at the back of their closet, saving it for when they get big. Kids must go through their own economic depression—wasting money and then not having any when they need it—to learn about money. In general, people best learn to save only after they've learned how to be broke.

Rule Four: As long as they're not engaged in illegal activity, allow children to spend, save, or waste the money any way they see fit. They can use it to hire others to do their chores. They can even hire a babysitter if they don't want to go somewhere with the family. But there's a catch: When it's gone, it's gone. No more allowance until the next week's envelope.

Jim's son, Charlie, learned a powerful lesson in money management the very first week he got on the allowance payroll. Their family visited a carnival, and the midway barkers had their way with the boy. He came home flat broke.

"Dad, what am I going to do for lunch?" Charlie said when reality struck him on Monday morning.

"Go over to your pay envelope and get your lunch money out," Jim replied.

"But it's all gone," Charlie said.

"Oh, no, that's really too bad. What are you going to do?" he said.

"I don't know," Charlie said. "Can I get some food out of the refrigerator and make a lunch?"

"Sure, if you can afford to pay for it," Jim said. "Mom and I have already paid for lunches once, and we don't want to pay for them again."

It was a tough week for Charlie. But surviving for five days on two meals a day (Jim and Shirley made sure they were good ones) taught him a big lesson in money management.

There will be times, however, when kids are more persistent—and more psychologically devious—than Charlie. When they blow their bankroll early and shuffle up to us begging for more money before the appointed allowance time, we must become as tight as a Depression-era banker. Sure, there will be more money—on the next allowance day. Even when our kids push the powerful guilt button, we must make sure nothing moves out of our pockets.

Observe how this dad handles daughter Jenna's midweek crisis:

JENNA: "Dad, I need more allowance."

DAD: "Yeah, that's kind of how it is for me. I always need more money in my paycheck than I get. Any idea what you're going to do?"

JENNA: "Yeah. I'm asking you. Dad, could you give me more allowance?"

DAD: "Well, I'll be happy to give you your allowance on Saturday. But for now, maybe you'll consider bidding on someone else's chores around the house so you can earn some money that way."

JENNA: "But I need it now!"

DAD: "Boy, I bet you do. But don't worry. You'll get more on Saturday."

JENNA: "That's not fair!"

DAD: "That could be true, and there will be more on Saturday."

JENNA: "My friends don't have this problem because their parents love them and give them more money."

DAD: "I bet that's true, too, *and* there will be more on Saturday."

If Jenna keeps it up, Dad could put a finishing touch to the discussion by saying, "If I kept carrying on like that with my boss, how do you suppose he'd feel about my job? He'd feel like paying me less, wouldn't he? So do your best to solve this, Jenna. We'll see you later."

Pearl 2

Anger: When It's Appropriate

As a general rule, the decision on whether or not to use anger in our dealings with our children hinges on the issue of separation of problems. Kids' problems should always be met with our empathy. They got themselves into the mess. The gain in their responsibility can be won only if we commiserate with them, not if we shout at them when they're working it out. If our kids' mistakes only hurt them and not us—if they throw their fists and come home with a black eye, or fail half a dozen classes at school—then our anger makes the problem worse. When our kids do something that affects us directly—lose our tools, leave their trikes in the driveway, fail to put our things away after using them—then it's okay for us to get a bit huffy. They will recognize that we're angry because their misbehavior has affected us.

Amanda, in her eagerness to cut out paper dolls, broke her mom's scissors. Mom, realizing that anger was entirely appropriate, said, "Amanda, I'm so angry I can't see straight. Now I can't even use my own scissors. I expect you to do something to make this right. Be prepared to tell me what you are going to do before you go to bed tonight." Notice that Mom did not demean the child with her anger; she didn't tell Amanda how stupid and irresponsible she was. Instead, she focused on how Amanda's action affected her and the need for a solution.

Anger is also generally appropriate if we've made a rational decision to use it. Occasionally, kids need to be read a sixty-second riot act. They need a show of anger. We can ponder these options: "Do I want to isolate my child? Or do I want to talk it over with him or her and do some problem solving? Or do I think this child needs a sixty-second rant and a hug afterward, with me saying, 'The reason I'm so angry, dear, is because you're the type of kid who could've handled the situation so much better.'"

The decision to use anger must be dispassionate, not a flying-off-the-handle, finger-poking-the-chest bawl-out. Generally speaking, anger should be used only when our children's behavior directly affects us, as using it often diminishes its effect.

Pearl 3

Bedtime

"Time for bed, sweetie." You say it every night. And every night you have to jump through all sorts of hoops before you get any action. It's always something: "After this program ends." "Can I have something to eat first?" "Read me a story." "But I'm not tired." "There are monsters in my room." When it comes to finding reasons for not crawling under the covers, every kid is an Einstein. The fact is, you cannot make children go to sleep. Their eyes will close and the dreams will descend on them when their body clocks tell them to. All the parental orders in the world can't make it happen.

The sad thing with many parents is that they put their children to bed simply to get them out of their hair in the evening. These parents say, "Mommy and Daddy are tired, so it's time for you kids to go to bed." Ideally, the children should be able to be awake and out of their parents' hair—at the same time. Instead of saying, "This is how much sleep you need every night," the Love and Logic parent says, "This is how much sleep you have an *opportunity* to get at night because you're in your room." That opportunity can begin at 7:30 or 8:30 or some other time. Allow the child and your need for privacy to determine the time. This takes the heat out of the bedtime battle. In fact, it makes it no battle at all.

Bedtime, like many other control issues, can be defused by giving up control. Parents tend to underestimate children's need for just a tiny bit of control. So when they see their kids going for all the control, they think that's what the children really want. In reality, all they want is a little control, not the whole enchilada.

So give it up. Ask your children if they'd rather have their door open or closed, their room light on or off, their night-light on or off, the radio on softly or off, and so on. Ask your kids if they'd like to hear a bedtime story first or not. Don't hold all the cards; cut them in on the action too.

A discussion of the bedtime issue with your child might go like this:

PARENT: "How much sleep do you think you need at night?"
CHILD: "Not very much. I like to be up at night."
PARENT: "Is that right? I can understand that. But you know, I'm the type of person who needs eight hours of sleep and about two hours of 'alone' time every night. So that's ten hours we won't be together."
CHILD: "Uh-huh."
PARENT: "Would you rather my 'alone' time start at 8:00 or at 8:30? Now, when I start my alone time, that means you need to be in your room. You can read if you want, or you can go to sleep. Which time would you prefer?"
CHILD: "I don't know."
PARENT: "Well, if you don't know, then I'll pick a time."
CHILD: "Okay, 8:30. Can I have my light on?"
PARENT: "Sure."
CHILD: "Can I play music?"
PARENT: "Yes, as long as I can't hear it."
CHILD: "Do I have to be in bed?"
PARENT: "Nope."
CHILD: "Can I sleep on the floor?"
PARENT: "No problem."

Many of us won't grant this sort of control for fear of the consequences. We're afraid that Brennan—up till 1:00 a.m. rocking with his radio and sorting his baseball cards—is going to be one obnoxious little dude in the morning. We're right, of course, but that doesn't mean Brennan has to be an obnoxious dude around us. It's the obnoxiousness we consequence, not the number of hours he sleeps. Don't think, *Now he's obnoxious; therefore, I've got to make him sleep more.* Do think, *He's obnoxious; therefore, I can provide him with a super learning experience.* Then say to the child, "You need to spend more time in your room because you're cranky."

The child will probably say, "Well, I didn't get enough sleep last night."

And your reply? "Good thinking." The lesson will hit home.

Pearl 4

Bossiness

Is it any wonder that bossy parents often have bossy kids? Parents who order their children around like boot-camp recruits end up with kids who want to be drill sergeants. It makes perfect sense. Little children love to act big. If they see the big people in their lives bossing, they'll boss too. So the first place to look for fault with bossy kids is ourselves. If we command our kids to jump and expect them to say, "How high?" our kids will be mirror images of us in their dealings with their playmates.

However, it's not always the parents who are at fault. Even non-bossy moms and dads sometimes have bossy kids. Oftentimes these children are simply addicted to having their own way, and bossing others is one way to accomplish that goal. Occasionally these control-conscious children will even turn their demanding mouths on us. *That* we won't tolerate. One way to handle this is to have a good one-liner ready for immediate use.

When the bossy bit happens, our first response is a genuine extended smile at the child. This unexpected turn of events gives him or her time to think, to wonder what in the world is going on. Then we say something like, "Nice try, Alicia. Nice try. What do you think happens in this family when people get really bossy? Does it help or not? But please don't answer that now. Just give it some thought." Then we walk off.

We deal with bossy children without injecting any emotion into the atmosphere. We also don't lay into them with, "Don't you *dare* order me around!" Their behavior is dealt with rationally and forthrightly. When our children boss other kids around, however, we become counselors. After all, now it's their problem, not ours.

> MOM: "Alicia, I notice that you're kind of bossy with those other kids. Do you ever worry that this might make them not like you? They wouldn't be your friends anymore then."
> ALICIA: "Aw, they'd still be my friends."
> MOM: "I just wonder how it'll work out. Of course, you might be one of those rare people who can boss others around and still make them be friends. What do you think? Have you figured out any ways you can boss them around and still keep them as friends?"
> ALICIA: "I don't know."
> MOM: "Well, I'll be interested to watch and see how it goes. I hope it works out for you."

Chances are that somewhere along the line it won't work out. The real world will drive the lesson home: Rudeness equals losing friends and making enemies. Other kids happily provide learning experiences for bossy kids like Alicia. Then when Alicia returns to Mom's side with her problem, Mom can express the sadness of a true friend:

> MOM: "Oh, so that really didn't work out, huh, Alicia?"
> ALICIA: "No."
> MOM: "That's really sad. What do you suppose you'll do to get your friends back?"
> ALICIA: "I don't know."
> MOM: "I sure hope that works out for you. If you ever decide you want me to give you some ideas about working with other kids so they don't feel bossed around, let me know. I'll be glad to talk to you about it."

Telling our kids not to be so bossy only bosses them and makes them mad at us, and the bossiness will continue. But putting the burden of the problem on their shoulders and always being nearby with a word of advice if it's asked for will push them toward a solution.

Pearl 5

Bullies

Since the first one-room schoolhouse, there have been children who bully others, but in days of yore, kids didn't bring guns to school to settle their disputes. Why do some kids get bullied more than others? The fact is that there are many good, quiet, polite, and intelligent kids who are mistreated by others, particularly in the zoo called middle—or junior high—school. (It should have been called "senior elementary," and then everyone would have more correct expectations.) Generally, preteens make fun of almost anyone or anything different. All the politically correct "celebrate diversity" speeches tend to fall on deaf ears in middle school and aren't going to change behavior that may be simply a developmental response at this stage of life.

Unfortunately, depending upon the school, being very good-looking, responsible, and kind leads some good kids to stand out like punching dummies—especially if they don't know how to easily roll with the give-and-take of preteen nonsense. Some children who relate well to adults and who are more mature simply have trouble coping with the immaturity of their peers.

Many parents attempt to make the *situation* kinder for their child. This may work. Sometimes a mom with a special-needs child can tell a class how much she and her child appreciate their understanding and how hard it is for the child to understand what is socially appropriate. The more challenged the child, the more important it is to try to modify the environment in this way. However, if the child is competent and understanding, it may be better to help him or her learn to cope.

Instead of modifying what goes on *outside* the skin, the parent helps the child grow and cope from what is happening on the *inside.* Naturally, if it is a case in which a child is in physical danger, the situation itself has to be modified.

A mom or dad might encourage their child by saying, "Kids who are awful now often grow up to be good men and women. Pretty surprising, isn't it? Someday they'll be almost as mature as you! Luckily, this is just a stage in their lives. I sure am proud of the way you handle it." Wise parents at least let the child know that being teased doesn't mean there is something wrong with him or her but that it's a problem the other children have.

Obviously, the more the children learn to handle this type of situation now, with an unshakable appreciation of their own "goodness" despite what others imply at school, the stronger men and women they will be and the less reliant they will be on peer decisions as they grow up. Early teasing provides children with an opportunity to learn both coping skills and the ability not to internalize the problems of others. A parent might say, "Honey, all your life you are going to be around fairly miserable people. Lucky for you, you are learning to handle that now. Some don't really understand how to cope until they are adults! I expect you'll come out of this wiser, more thoughtful, and more understanding of others for learning this now."

The things that often don't work are:

- Trying to make the environment more accepting (although if a child is being truly threatened, school officials must step in and remove the offenders).
- Trying to "build the child up" with false affirmation or phony praise.
- Giving unasked-for advice and suggestions on behavior.
- Showing how much you hurt for the child and how frustrated and helpless you feel in the situation.

Pearl 6

Car Wars: Backseat Battles

It starts benignly. Cameron trespasses into Molly's "space" in the backseat of the family car, and Molly yells, "Mom, Cameron's on my side." Then Molly socks him on the arm. "Keep your filthy paws on your own side, Cameron!"

Cameron retreats to his armrest to regroup, for Molly is marginally larger than he and packs a meaner right jab. But the provocateur in Cameron cannot be subdued. Carefully, he inches his right hand toward the middle of the seat. First his forefinger, then the rest of his fingers, then his whole hand moves into his sister's space.

"Mom!" Molly yells. "Make him stop!" Then she attacks: fists, screams, hair pulling. World War III breaks out in the backseat.

There is something about the backseat of a moving car that excites kids. Call it cabin fever, call it seizing the moment when parents are otherwise occupied, but put two or more kids in the same car together, and they turn into a cross between guerrilla warriors and stool pigeons. They fight, they argue, they hassle each other, and they hassle us. So we say, "You guys be quiet back there." While this may provide temporary relief, it usually fails to have a lasting effect. In fact, it may last only a few blocks, at which point we are forced to say something even stronger.

The backseat problem is one we can and should nip in the bud. If we handle the problem when it's not really serious, it will never become serious. But we must choose the time wisely: when we aren't in a hurry to get anywhere and when it doesn't matter how long we take to get our message across. Our message is simply, "I'm not going to tolerate backseat bickering, and if it continues, *something* is going to happen."

Consider the following for kids who are in grade school:

Lance was ready for anything his backseat warriors could hit him with one morning. He had rehearsed his lines and even brought a paperback with him to kill the time he expected to be wasting on the trip.

Right on schedule, his kids started going at each other in the backseat. Lance stopped the car, turned very calmly around, and said, "You know, guys, I think the hard thing about being cooped up in a tiny car like this is that the oxygen level in your blood gets low and then you get irritated and fight. But if you can get out of the car and replenish it, things always get better. Why don't you guys get out of the car and work your problem out and replenish your oxygen level at the same time? I'll just drive ahead and wait for you."

As protection for his kids, Lance added, "Now, if you don't walk too close to the cars going down the street, and if you stay on the sidewalk, I'm sure you'll be safe and you won't get hit."

Then he drove up the street several blocks to a place where his kids could see him, parked the car, and read his book. He could see them jawing at each other and getting on each other's case as they walked. But as they neared the car, they got better and better. By the time they got to the car, they were calm.

As one child reached for the door handle and started to open the door, the other jumped in front and the war resumed. So Lance pulled up another few blocks and parked there to read his book. When his kids got there, they were in pretty good shape.

Now whenever he drives down the road and his kids start to get rowdy, he simply says, "Hey, guys, are you needing to replenish the oxygen supply?" and his kids pipe down right away.

Here's another idea for handling backseat bickering:

Stacey called her best friend one evening to explain her problem and ask for a favor: "Can you follow my car on Saturday morning at 11:30 and just do a little FBI surveillance for me? Stay a few car lengths back. When we get to Third and Main, I'm sure I'm going to be throwing a couple of kids out of the car. I've always been afraid of doing this before because the kids might get kidnapped or something, but I'd have the confidence to do it if you were watching them and making sure they were safe."

Next morning, true to form, by the time Stacey's car reached First and Main, the kids were screaming like little monkeys in too small of a cage. Stacey said, "Guys, I can't drive with that noise. It hassles my mind."

The kids hit the volume knob. They knew Mom wasn't going to do anything—she never had before—and they felt safe no matter how loud they got.

Stacey gave them another chance to amend their ways. "Hey, guys!" she yelled over the commotion. "I can't drive with that noise." It was to no avail.

So right at Third and Main, Stacey pulled the car over, went around to the other side of the car, and opened the kids' door. "We can't walk home," they said. "We'll be kidnapped."

But Stacey hung tough. This was, after all, what her rehearsal had been for. She said, "Keep your eyes down. Don't look up, and maybe nobody will bother you. I'll see you at home." And she took off.

Later her friend told her, "You didn't need me. You should have seen those kids walking home. They looked so somber. They never did look up."

You can bet Stacey's kids listen to her now. If we can pull one of these tactics when there is no hurry to get anywhere, then when we are in a hurry, one little word directed toward the backseat will get the results we are after.

We would like to provide some additional clarification about this Pearl, which involves risk that some parents will see as acceptable and others will not. Society as a whole has become more protective. Children must be in car seats until they are seven; because of child labor laws, a school-age child can't legally help his dad in the family business; no child can be expelled easily from school for disrupting the studies of other children. Society hasn't made it easy for parents to take even small, thoughtful risks to teach children important lessons. Years ago, children were generally well mannered when going out to eat, as almost all children expected to wait out the meal sitting in the family car if their behavior was such that they were bothering others around them.

Now few American parents would ever risk allowing their children to sit in a car in a well-lit parking lot, in front of the restaurant, within direct eyesight of the parents. Times have changed!

With this Pearl, we are not encouraging parents to put their children in dangerous situations. In the examples given, precautions that ensure the children's safety are noted. And when putting a child out of the car to walk home, naturally, the length of the walk is based upon the age of the child, the traffic in the area, the dangerousness of the neighborhood, and so on. When a parent is concerned about allowing a very young or impulsive child to walk a few blocks home, that's correct and understandable. But it is just plain sad when a parent is too fearful to allow his or her child the opportunity of the learning experience of walking a few blocks home when the family lives in a quiet neighborhood in a state of ten million in which one kidnapping a decade occurs.

Pearl 7

Chores

Nothing warms the heart like the sight of our children industriously flitting about the house completing their chores. We see them assuming a sense of responsibility and belonging, and we are right proud. Plus, there's work being done, progress being made, and our property being cared for. Oh, happy, happy day!

Come now, this isn't utopia. More commonly, chores are dreaded—by parents and youngsters alike. The fact is, hands don't shoot up in giddy excitement when we ask, "Who wants to do the dishes?" Happy feet don't scurry for the broom when we ask, "Okay, who wants to clean the garage today?" But if handled properly, we *can* take the hassle out of chores. And we start when our kids are young.

When they are little, kids enjoy doing things with their parents. We say "doing things with" instead of "helping" because, face it, what they do is *not* real help. They just naturally like to copy us. They like to stir around in the water as Mom does dishes. They like to push around their little lawn mowers when Dad cuts the grass. When it snows, they cry rivers if we don't buy them little plastic shovels so they can "help" scoop the walks. (Too bad they don't do that when they're twelve!)

The secret to instilling a good attitude in our kids about chores (brace yourself, this may sound like bad news) is that *we* must have fun while doing them. If we make it seem like drudgery, then our little ones will think, *If that is what doing chores is like, count me out.* Getting them to do anything around the house for the next twelve to fourteen years will resemble arms negotiations. So during the toddler years, we should get the idea across that work is fun. Wise parents will say things like,

- "I sure like getting my jobs done around the house. It's fun for me!"
- "Wow, do I ever enjoy doing things with you!"
- "We sure have fun together!"

As kids reach an age when they can be held responsible—kindergarten or first grade—they should be given some very elementary tasks around the house, like cleaning up messes they make, helping clean their rooms, and making their beds (although not up to hospital standards). By third grade and throughout the rest of grade school, they're ready to periodically wash dishes, vacuum the family room, sweep out the garage, take out the trash, wipe out the refrigerator, and help clean dirty windows and the car (inside and out).

However, there will be static. Kids have nimble minds. They will find excuses for not doing their chores, or they'll argue about who does what, or they'll complain about when they have to do them.

Love and Logic parents negotiate with their children on chores. They tack a list of all chores onto a prominent place in the kitchen and then ask their kids to read it and decide which chores they would most like to do. A day or two later, the whole family sits down to divvy them up. Rather than the parents deciding who does what, allow the kids themselves that control. If the chores are distributed unfairly, for whatever reason, the "unfaired upon" kid will quickly smell a con job and request renegotiation.

Foster's kids once sat down to divide up chores. What seemed to be a very inequitable arrangement was agreed to between Jerry, age fifteen, and Melinda, age eleven. The chores were: feeding the dog and doing dishes. The dog food was in the basement, and because Melinda was afraid of the dark, she opted for doing dishes every day instead of testing the unseen terrors of the basement. It didn't take long, however, for Melinda to see the unfair division of labor—and to overcome her fear of the dark. A renegotiation of jobs came about. Kids will work out chore problems between them when they're given some control.

A bigger problem is getting the chores done on your time schedule. Wise parents establish a time frame with phrases like "By the next time you eat" or "By the time I take you to your soccer game." That way the child always knows the ground rules.

One sort of parent who ends up with resistant kids is the "Oh, by the way" parent. The simple sight of a child sitting in a chair reading sends these parents into deep flights of remembering. They remember all the jobs around the house that haven't been done—jobs that haven't even been assigned.

The "Oh, by the way" parents say things like, "Oh, by the way, can you pick up the trash in the yard?" or "Oh, by the way, can you polish the grillwork on the car?" Foster's mom pulled this on him when he was young, and he ended up doing his reading in the furnace room!

PEARL 8

Church: When Kids Don't Want to Go

Responsible parents want to bring their children up with established spiritual values. They want their kids to have faith, understand the Christian message, and know God intimately. That means involving the family in a church and its activities. Unfortunately, there comes a time in our children's lives when they don't want to go to church. They have to sit still for so long. They don't really understand what the guy up front is talking about. Their Sunday clothes make them feel like there's an army of ants loose in the linings.

A more serious reason for many kids' dislike of church is rebellion against parental values.[7] Children learn early in life that their parents can't get into their brains. We can't make them think what we think or believe what we believe. When we try, we invite their disobedience; the kids see us usurping control, and they want to grab some of it back. This is another area of parenting in which proper modeling is vital. If, from our children's infancy on, we have spoken positively about going to church—oftentimes to each other, but within earshot of the children—we will have encouraged our kids, without coercion, to like going to church. We want to make genuine, well-placed statements like, "I'm sure glad I have my church. I enjoy my friends and always get such needed encouragement while I'm there," or, "I always feel a lot better when I go to church. It really helps me keep my values in place." Positive statements can set the bug in our kids' ears and lessen their inclination to rebel.

At some point, however, our kids may dig in their heels and make a stand. It is often valuable to attempt to uncover the reasons for their displeasure with church. Maybe they don't care for their Sunday school teacher, or they've had the Baby Moses story for the past six years running and are bored stiff, or there are few kids their age. It could be any number of things. Talking it out with our kids may help them see the value of Sunday morning time with God.

And, of course, there are always ways to make our children go to church—tactics we don't advise. By using these tactics, we do not allow our kids to appreciate and value the experience of their own volition. We can exert our power and feel in control, or we can look for a creative long-term solution. The important thing to remember is that parental demands will probably come to fruition in rebellion. Kids will fight parents who insist, "You *have to* believe what I believe."

But have faith. Disliking church is most likely a stage. As little kids, they love Sunday school. Then comes the phase when they don't want to go. However, if we haven't made church attendance a major issue during the early years—presenting a good role model instead—our kids will most likely see value in going to church as they get older.

Pearl 9

Creativity

A creative child is a fun-to-be-around child. Children's creativity fills us with a strange mixture of surprise, joy, and pride. Truly creative children are self-stimulating. They are motivated to accomplish on their own. Creativity is a "doing" concept. No one can be creative while watching a football game or watching TV. Creative children don't whine, "What can I do?" and "What can I watch?"

However, creativity is best when combined with self-discipline. If you have a creative child who has no self-discipline, then you have raised "the child from hell." After all, it is creative to paint on top of wallpaper, color the dog with nail polish, and shoot colored ink onto the ceiling with a water pistol. Self-discipline and creativity are not related and are independent variables. Self-disciplined children can be either creative or not. And creative children can be self-disciplined or not. The kids who are a real joy are creative and self-disciplined!

Encouraging Creativity in Early Toddlerhood

Creativity is strongly related to inquisitiveness. Toddlerhood is the most important time for parents to encourage their children's curiosity. During these foundation years, the brain is very malleable and its growth is completely dependent on environmental givens and expectations. Amazingly, the brain is physically changed by what takes place during infancy and toddlerhood.

Two to six are the ages of industry and initiative. Wise parents encourage their children to explore the environment. Sadly, I often see a toddler exploring the environment in an airport waiting area or the church narthex, not bothering anybody, and then one of his parents discourages him by saying, "Come here," when the child isn't going anyplace anyway. I feel sorry for both the child and the parent. Let the kid go. Let him explore. As long as he isn't intruding on another's space or tranquility, relax!

During toddlerhood, wise parents excite their children by showing enthusiasm about exploring and understanding the world. A parent might blow on a mobile: "What makes that go around?" And, looking at a candle, "Wow, when that gets hot, it bubbles." Toddlers love learning how to work the buttons on the DVD player and the TV. They want to know how high they can stack blocks and how cream mixes with coffee when it is stirred. Curiosity and creativity wind around each other. Wise parents are forever saying, "Wow, look at that! How does that work?"

Discipline, as we said in the beginning, is an essential element for happiness with the curious child. Only discipline leads to a joyful exploring of the environment that is fun for both parent and child. It's only enjoyable to have a toddler explore the waiting room or narthex if he will come when called, and only fun to have a child watch how coffee mixes with cream if he respects the adult's wishes that he not grab the cup. Recently, I (Foster) was in a home where the kids were designing the Snake River Drainage Basin all over the kitchen floor. I asked their mother about the watery mess the kids were making in front of the refrigerator and stove, and she laughed, saying, "Well, the kitchen floor is made to be wet. And it works because they clean it up as soon as I ask!"

Encouraging Creativity in Early Childhood

The easiest way to encourage creativity in early childhood is to deep-six the TV. But that's almost impossible for young parents who grew up with TV themselves during their formative years. But it is probably sufficient to say that all children should spend more time *doing* something at home than *watching* something. The following is a partial list of how parents have encouraged creativity in early childhood:

- Use a thrift shop as your toy store and buy clocks and all sorts of mechanical stuff to take apart; clothes for dress-up; and old jewelry boxes to store and collect important stuff. Start your child's collection of anything fun—old postcards, salt and pepper shakers, or padlocks.
- Make sure you have a white wall covered with plastic for dry marker drawings.
- Every home would be better off with a built-in stage than a built-in media center.
- In addition to reading stories to your children, make up stories round-robin fashion.
- Make sure that, in Mary Poppins style, every job has an element of fun.

Encouraging Creativity in Childhood

Childhood is the time when the entrepreneurs and inventors of the future really start to bloom. Parents encourage this by showing excitement around their child's areas of strength. These are the years of exposure to the wonders of the world—exposure to museums, art shows, plays, and dinner theaters. Whatever the child is exposed to, it is most effective if the parents are excited about the experience too. Whatever activities the parents experience with joy, in the company of their children, the children take up with relish and, after a time, usually become absorbed in it without parental input. My own mom interested my brother and me in darkrooms, guppy breeding, butterfly collecting, and writing by being excited about all of these activities for a short time and then turning the darkroom, aquariums, butterfly nets, and typewriters over to us. Her motto was "Try it—you'll probably like it!" And her love coupled with her excited curiosity about the world has lasted us for three quarters of a century.

In summary, show excitement about how things work, do things with your children, become excited about what they and you discover, and you will probably raise self-motivated, curious, and creative children.

Pearl 10

Crisis Situations

Drug use. Kids who run away from home. Teenage pregnancy. Debilitating injury. Suicide. A death in the family. A crippling disease. Divorce. When a crisis hits our lives or the lives of our children, it can send us reeling. Guilt, worry, anxiety, anger, and inconsolable grief are some of the emotions that can stagger us.

One of the most damaging ideas we carry into a crisis situation is that something must be done right now. This is seldom true. The character denoting crisis in the Chinese language is a combination of the symbols for danger and opportunity. We see the danger all too well, but we often miss the opportunity.

The following four thoughts may help us deal with a crisis:

> ***First, crises, by their very nature, are generally temporary.*** There are usually better times ahead. Knowing this, we can guard against over-involvement.
>
> ***Second, almost no crisis must be dealt with immediately.*** We usually have time to pray, think, and act rationally, and seek advice from others who have had a similar experience or are professionally capable of dealing with it.
>
> Also, many of what we perceive to be crises are not crises at all. The problem may have been going on for months or even years and becomes a crisis only when we find out about it. So we need to adopt the proper mindset. If we suddenly discover that

our child has been taking drugs, this is a serious happening, true, but it's not necessarily a crisis. We have time to take care of it properly. (Of course, if recent drug ingestion appears to present the possibility of death, severe illness, or brain damage if medical support is not given immediately, *that* is a crisis.)

We may even want to consider doing nothing about the crisis. Granted, in many cases, this is not a good solution, but we should still consider the option. Just doing *something* is not the answer; doing the *right* thing is.

After writing all the options down—from the most active response to the least—we should talk them over with someone we respect. A clear perspective is key.

Third, to help us cope, we must always ask ourselves what the worst possible outcome of the crisis would be. Many times we find we are able to deal with that.

Sometimes the worst possibly outcome is death, and even *that* must be faced by *all* people sometime. Naturally, it feels good to put it off a bit. But if a person dies suddenly, without warning, it is no crisis for that person. And even the loved ones who are left have a choice of considering the situation either a "crisis" that needs to be taken care of immediately or a "terrible and painful happening" that needs to be thought (and felt) through.

Finally, we always need to keep the monkey on the back of the person responsible for the problem. Sometimes that is difficult. For instance, if our child is using drugs, that can be a problem for parents if the family car is crashed or money is stolen from the family to pay for the habit. Nevertheless, even in such circumstances some parents act as if the whole thing is their problem, whereas others still manage to look at their child and communicate, "Honey, *you* have a big problem" and then go on to do whatever they need to do to take care of themselves.

In summary, when a crisis erupts, we should take a moment, pray, breathe deeply, relax, write down all possible options and talk them over with a person we respect, think about our ability to cope with the worst possible outcome, and keep the faith. After all, faith is our best weapon.

Pearl 11

Discipline 101

The key to effective discipline is to control only what we can control. We can never make an infant stop crying, quit bothering us, stop sucking his or her thumb, or cut the whining. What we can and should control, though, is *where* he or she does all these things. If our children ignore our firm "Please stop" once, with no pleading or whining on our part, then they should be given the opportunity to act obnoxiously someplace else—and that place is in their room. But remember, we are not sending them there to punish them; we are merely giving them the opportunity to pull themselves together. If they come out still angry and obnoxious, we send them back to stay an added five minutes for every year of their age.

We should *never* forget to show love to our kids. When their good mood returns, they need to be hugged and rocked for doing things right. Also, keep in mind these three common mistakes that surface during discipline sessions:

> ***First, we can be too tough.*** Little kids are, at times, no fun. Aren't we all? Remember, everyone has a right to be crabby and moody at times—even our kids. For example, if we've kept our young child up far past the normal bedtime and he or she is a total grump the next day, is it fair for us to sentence the child to solitary confinement? Understanding and common sense go a long way in parent-child relationships.

Second, we can be too lenient, putting up with too much before we issue the "Go" command. Too much malarkey stretches our tolerance, and by the time we say "*Adios*" to our child, we may be angry rather than effective.

Third, we may confuse anger with firmness. Firm people may be loud, or may even use a little physical pressure, but firm, I-mean-business people don't yell and scream, and they seldom show frustration.

Here are nine rules that apply particularly to controlling an out-of-control kindergartner or first-grader:

1. Avoid all physical tussles. For instance, small mothers should not try to maneuver big children to their rooms.
2. Use orders sparingly. Never give a child an order you cannot make him or her follow.
3. Tell your child what you wish he or she would do rather than giving an order.
4. Give a complete "I message": "I would appreciate your going to your room now so I can feel better about you and me." ("I messages" tell why you feel that way.)
5. Sometimes when a request is given, it is wise to thank the child in advance, anticipating compliance.
6. When the child is in a good mood, talk things over, exploring his or her feelings and laying down expectations for the future.
7. Use isolation or a change of location for behavior problems rather than trying to stop the behavior.
8. When things are done right, be emotional. When things are done poorly, be nonemotional, matter-of-fact, and consequential.
9. If you cannot deal with the situation on your own immediately, delay the consequences and recruit ideas and reinforcements from others. Then use your time to find a solution that will both be effective and fit the crime. Some

people wrongly concern themselves with the possibility of the child forgetting what he or she has done. This is usually not a problem. The ultimate value of delaying the consequence is for the parent, not the child. It gives the parent time to think and plan.

Here's how Lisa uses these rules to send her five-year-old son, Blake, to his room:

BLAKE: "Mom, come here right now!"
LISA: "Hey, kiddo, I don't like it when you talk to me that way. I'd like you to scoot up to your room and give it some thought."
BLAKE: "No! I'm not going!"
LISA: "Blake, I would like you to go to your room."
BLAKE: "No!"
LISA: "Blake, I think you are making a poor choice."
BLAKE: "You can't make me go."
LISA: "I don't want to make you. You are making a poor choice. It would be wise for you to go to your room now."
BLAKE: "No!"
LISA: "Well, I'm disappointed. I wish you had given it more careful thought. I will have to do something else about this, but not right now. I will get back to you on it. Try not to worry."

Lisa failed, right? Wrong. She merely handled what she could handle. She refrained from spanking. She didn't carry the boy to his room, as he was too big. She also didn't issue an order she couldn't enforce. All of her comments were "I messages"—things she could do, not telling the child what he should do. Correct moves. But she didn't get results. So later she enlisted the support of her husband, Eric. Lisa talked the situation over with him when he returned home from work, and then they engaged Blake in the following discussion at the dinner table:

ERIC: "How did the day go, honey?"
LISA: "Oh, pretty good. But Blake had trouble going to his room."

ERIC: "You're kidding?"

LISA: "No, it's a fact, dear."

ERIC: "Well, do you think he needs practice, honey?"

BLAKE: "I don't need practice. I know how to do it."

ERIC: "You know that when your mother says move, you should move."

BLAKE: "All right, all right."

ERIC: "How much practice does he need, honey? A hundred trips?"

LISA: "No, I think probably twenty from here to his room will do. We don't want to give him more practice than he needs. Blake's a fairly smart kid."

ERIC: "Okay, Blake, you can finish your dinner after you've made twenty trips to and from your room. Start now! Fast!"

BLAKE: "But . . ."

ERIC: "How do I want you to go?"

BLAKE: "Fast."

ERIC: "How do I want you to move?"

BLAKE: "Fast!"

ERIC: "Thank you. Now move out."

BLAKE: "Okay, I'm going. I'm going."

Notice that when Lisa was dealing with Blake, she didn't cut herself down. She didn't say, "Wait until your dad gets home." On the contrary, she stayed in charge the whole time. Later she was even kind, cutting the practice during the dinnertime training session.

As for Eric, he was extremely firm without losing his self-control. He said what he meant, and he meant what he said. Most important, he backed his wife to the hilt. He didn't allow Blake to drive a wedge between Lisa and him.

Pearl 12

Discipline in Public

Kids are born smart. Even before they can speak intelligibly, they know when to apply the needle to us. More times than not, their bigger triumphs are in a store, a shopping center, a restaurant, and other public places.

You've been there. Put little Caitlin in your shopping cart, and she launches into her fire engine imitation. Take your eyes off little Anthony for one second at church, and before you know it, he's chewing on Mrs. Snyder's nylons three rows away. If you scold them, they let out a wail that makes Mick Jagger sound like a member of the Vienna Boys Choir.

As one mother put it, "Julia behaves just great when we happen to be going somewhere she wants to go, but just let it be a shopping trip for me, and the kid goes wild. It always seems to happen in a public place, where I just can't gain control of the situation. Everybody stares at us, and I'm so embarrassed, I could die."

Kids think their parents don't dare do anything to them because they're out in public. Parents think they don't dare consequence their kids with so many people looking on. However, the people watching wonder why in the world those parents don't do something about that obnoxious kid!

When you put it all together, it can get pretty hairy. But a public place is no different from the living room. True, it doesn't lend itself to meaningful parent-child discussion, but that doesn't mean we just forget Love and Logic principles. Children who misbehave in a public place must be disciplined; otherwise, every trip to the store sets the stage for disaster.

One technique for breaking this bad habit is called "Strategic Training Session." It is somewhat involved and requires planning and cooperation from friends or family members. Done once, the lesson will take, and public kid-attacks will be a thing of the past.

Heather tried it with her seven-year-old daughter, Phoebe. She phoned her best friend one evening and said, "I've been having trouble with Phoebe when I go shopping, and I need your help. Would you station yourself at the pay phone outside Wal-Mart tomorrow morning at 10:30? I have a feeling you're going to get a call." Heather then filled her friend in on the plan.

The next day, Heather and Phoebe went shopping, and true to form, Phoebe became her usual obnoxious self even before the automatic doors of the store had closed behind them. In a quiet voice, Heather said, "Phoebe, would you rather behave or go sit in your room?"

Phoebe looked quizzically at her mom as if to say, "Get real, Mom. You'd take me home after you've come all the way down here to shop?" Then she ratcheted her attack up a notch. The next thing Phoebe knew, she was being led to a pay phone near the front of the store, where Heather dialed a number and said, "Shopping is not fun today. Please come." Thirty seconds later, Phoebe's eyes grew as big as pie plates when her mom's friend strolled through the door, took Phoebe's hand, and said, "Let's go to your room. You can wait for your mom there."

Phoebe was escorted home and sent to her room. Heather could then make her rounds in unharried bliss. Phoebe was allowed out of her room when Heather returned. She was very happy to see her mom again, while Heather was friendly and pleasant because she'd had a great time shopping. Heather taught her little girl that obnoxious behavior has consequences.

Strategic training sessions can be arranged with a spouse or even an older sibling. It is not necessary to take the misbehaving child home—to the car is far enough. There is absolutely no reason for our kids to get away with hellish behavior in public. One or at most two strategic training sessions can cure this problem.

PEARL 13

Divorce and Visitation

When parents divorce, the casualty list includes more than the husband and wife. Kids suffer too. They may experience mood swings, defensiveness about being touched, elimination problems (younger children), hyperactivity (grade-school children), back talk (teenagers), and general problems with schoolwork, lack of interest, and laziness. Such behavior is often part of a normal grieving process and can be alleviated by following these ten guidelines for divorced or divorcing parents. (Remember that there is no way to make it good for the kids. In their eyes, divorce is a disaster. These guidelines are offered as a way to make a bad situation a little better.)

Guideline One: Expect children to handle the divorce about as well as the adults handle it. If the parents are bitter, angry, and noncommunicative, the children will probably behave in much the same way.

Guideline Two: Let the children know that the divorce is not their fault. As adults, we know children seldom cause divorces. Nevertheless, some children may think, *If I had been a better kid, my parents wouldn't be divorcing.* A parent can say, "Isaac, you know that some kids are friends and then decide they can't get along. Well, that's kind of what has happened with Dad and me. But we both still love you."

Guideline Three: Be honest about feelings and observations. Parents need to tell their children, without details, how they feel about the ex-spouse and why. It is also helpful to give the other parent's point of view. But bad-mouthing the ex-spouse backfires.

Guideline Four: Understand children's misbehavior without excusing it. Encourage your children to express their feelings, but continue to give consequences for misbehavior. Parents must never tolerate disrespect.

Guideline Five: Give children a support group. Children need someone outside the family to talk with—school counselors, teachers, peer groups, or friends of the family.

Guideline Six: Post-divorce counseling for parents and children may help. When communication is poor and distrust rampant between the adults, counseling is almost always helpful, especially if both adults would really like things to improve.

Guideline Seven: Don't use your children to gain information. No matter how tempted you are to interrogate your children regarding your ex-spouse, it is generally best to refrain. Children sometimes give their parent answers he or she wants to hear. They can figure out what the parent is looking for. If one parent is looking for evidence that the other is a jerk, the kids will feed that desire.

Guideline Eight: Handle visitation issues directly with the ex-spouse. It is never wise to send messages to the ex-partner through the kids. If you want that person to know something, contact him or her directly.

Guideline Nine: Children need "moms" and "dads." In the case of a remarriage, it is best to encourage children to call stepparents "Mom" and "Dad." Kids won't forget who the "real" parent is. It's important to offer the children this option but not force the issue. Foster remembers a time in therapy when the child said, "I always wanted to call Susan "Mom" but I was never really sure she wanted me to." What to call the authority figures should at least be discussed.

Guideline Ten: In the case of a remarriage, the birth parent must completely back the stepparent in discipline. The parent must let the child know that his or her new spouse is a lifetime partner.

Divorce occurs in just over half of our families today. While this is regrettable, it should be faced honestly and used as an opportunity to learn how to help our children develop coping skills. Sometimes parents worry about *when* to tell their children about an impending divorce, but *when* is not nearly as important as *how* the children are told.

Overdoing apologies indicates guilt. Not surprisingly, many children take advantage of guilt-ridden adults. A guilty-sounding parent may unknowingly be conveying, "If it weren't for my problems, you wouldn't be acting this way, so you have every reason to complain, treat me with disrespect, and behave inappropriately." Instead, Love and Logic parents are not overly apologetic.

In talking with our kids about divorce, we might follow the example of how this mother counseled her daughter Courtney:

MOM: "So, Courtney, do you think you'll be affected by the divorce, or will it have no effect on you?"
COURTNEY: "I think it's pretty bad."
MOM: "Why's that?"
COURTNEY: "I don't want you to get divorced from Dad."
MOM: "But you know we fight all the time."
COURTNEY: "Yeah, but I try to be good so you won't fight."
MOM: "Do you think we fight over you not being good, or do we fight over other things?"
COURTNEY: "I don't know."
MOM: "Well, I want you to know that your dad and I do fight

a lot, but frankly, most of it isn't over you. We'd be getting a divorce even if we'd never had children. You know this divorce makes me feel troubled."

COURTNEY: "I don't want you to be upset."

MOM: "Well, I am, honey. I thought I would be married to your dad for life. But we'll make sure you still see him a lot, so you don't have to be upset just because I'm upset. You can decide for yourself how you're going to feel."

The message divorcing parents should send to their kids is, "This isn't going to wreck your life. I know you can handle it. It might be hard, but we will all be okay." The kids will have a much easier time if the parents are positive.

Using Love and Logic Between Two Homes

Unfortunately, when kids have two homes because of divorce, discussions like the following happen all too often:

JEN: "Dan, how could you let me down like this again? I think you do these things just to undermine what I'm trying to do with our daughter! You know exactly why I had to tell her she couldn't drive for a month. Nicole took my car without permission and stayed out all night. I was worried sick! You said you would support me by not letting her drive, and then you turned around and gave her your extra car to drive. How are we supposed to make her responsible if you reverse every decision we make?"

DAN: "Now, Jen, you don't have to be so upset. I was going to call you and tell you I think you're overreacting on this. She's just a kid, for Pete's sake! What she's doing is just typical teenage stuff. You need to cut her a little slack. Maybe if you'd lighten up a little, you'd both be a lot happier."

JEN: "Wait just a minute, Dan! That kind of behavior might be typical for some teenagers, but it's not how all teens act. She's crossed way over the line lately, and it's getting worse all the time. She doesn't feel that she has any limits at all, and I can see why. Every time she misbehaves, you're there to excuse it away and turn me into the bad guy for trying to hold her accountable for her actions."

Here we see two divorced parents embroiled in a classic struggle. It could be competition for Nicole's love on Dan's part, but it probably goes deeper than that. Dan is a caring man who doesn't like conflict. He lives to make sure that his daughter is always happy. Playing the role of the good guy is easy for him. It fits right into his lifelong pattern of conflict avoidance. It also helps him deal with his fear of losing Nicole to her mother.

Jen, on the other hand, is left with helping their daughter grow into a mature, responsible person. She knows that this can happen only if she sets limits and holds Nicole accountable for her actions, but this is difficult for her, as it often puts her in the role of the bad guy. In spite of this dilemma, she tries to hold the line with Nicole even in the face of unintentional, but very damaging, acts of sabotage by her ex-husband.

Both Jen and Dan are making several mistakes that continue to lock all three into a vicious cycle: Nicole misbehaves, Jen punishes, and Dan overturns the punishment.

Dan's Mistakes: Dan is willing to sacrifice Nicole's long-term happiness and quality of life in exchange for her short-term happiness. He fears the loss of Nicole's love and lives with the mistaken idea that she will appreciate and respect him in the role of her protector. Overturning his ex-wife's discipline also gives him a chance to make Mom look bad. He doesn't realize that Nicole may eventually view him with contempt for sabotaging her relationship with Mom.

Jen's Mistakes: Jen holds on to a fantasy that she and Dan are a team. If she couldn't get him to cooperate when they were married, what are the chances that this will happen after they've lived through the pain of divorce? Even though it's unlikely that Dan will suddenly change his tune and begin to back Jen's discipline, she holds on to the hope that he will.

Based upon this false idea, Jen imposes consequences that must be upheld when her daughter is at Dan's house. This gives Dan both the opportunity and the power to rescind the punishment and place himself in the role of Nicole's hero.

Jen's primary mistake is believing that she can make both homes work the same. This is one of the tragedies of divorce. All the energy she uses trying to make this happen is energy that can be spent on things she can actually control. Another mistake is trying to reason with Dan about this problem. Her discussions with Dan only give him yet another opportunity to attack her parenting attempts, and the worse the problem gets.

Jen's Solution: Once Jen realizes that Dan won't support her rules and consequences for Nicole, she can quit asking him for something he is unable or unwilling to give. This means she will start imposing consequences that are carried out only during the time in which Nicole is staying at her home. This puts her back in control and reduces some of her disappointment and resulting anger over not being supported. She needs to practice the following statement and use it often:

> Dan, in the past I have made the mistake of trying to make your home run like my home. I promise not to do that anymore. I won't tell you how to handle Nicole when she is with you. If I see her needing discipline when she is with me, I'll handle it here without asking you to deal with it while she's at your place. And you are welcome to do the same.

Her next step is to share her love and her thoughts with Nicole. Because their relationship is strained, it is unlikely that Mom can get all of her thoughts out without facing a counterattack. Teens are experts at arguing each point until what starts out as a discussion soon becomes a fight.

The solution is for Jen to put her thoughts in writing. Notice how her letter begins with a wonderful attention-getting strategy.

> Dear Nicole,
>
> I need to apologize to you. I'm doing it in writing just in case you want to revisit my thoughts in the future. Please don't feel a need to respond right away. I just want you to think about this for a while.

I have made a big mistake not being open with you about the fact that your dad and I often differ on how to be parents. I have spent too much time trying to make him be the same as me. That's not fair to you or to him. We both love you very much but have different ways of showing it. By trying to make him do things my way, you have been caught in the middle of our unhappiness. This often happens in marriages and especially happens in divorces.

My way of showing my love for you is to work hard to help you become a good person. To do this, I have to hold you accountable for your actions. This means I also have to be prepared for you to be angry with me for a while.

The mistake I have been making is to ask your dad to discipline you over things that happen in my house. I'm not going to do that anymore. You and I will take care of those problems without involving Dad. Dad can deal with any problems that come up at his house without interference from me. I hope this will be less confusing for you.

You are growing up with two different kinds of parents. As time goes on, you will have plenty of different thoughts and feelings about each of us. Please remember that we both love you very much. I hope you know the divorce was not your fault. I hope you know it's okay to love both Dad and me at the same time.

Love,
Mom

This was a tough letter for Mom to write. There were many things she wanted to say but knew better. She wanted to share her feelings of anger and hurt toward Dan. She felt a twinge of desire to tell Nicole how irresponsible she believes Dan to be. She wanted to scream out, "Your dad is messing up your life! Look at me! I'm the one who *really* cares!"

Instead, Jen walked the much healthier and nobler path. Why? Because she realizes that each time she criticizes Dan, she drives Nicole further away. Even though Dad rescues and excuses Nicole from her poor decisions, he's an important part of her life. If Mom were to bad-mouth him, it would do much more damage than his rescuing behavior. Nicole will learn some positive things from Dad, and from Mom she will learn how to take good care of herself and be responsible. Mom's staying out of the blame game will allow Nicole to sit back, watch her parents, and gather what's good from each. After all, isn't that what we all want for our kids?

Naturally, if, for example, the mother provides the child more rules or is forceful about higher expectations, the child will often say, "I like Dad's place better." Human nature pines for freedom—even the freedom to be self-destructive. A loving parent needs to assure her child by recognizing the feelings, explaining the situation, and sticking to her guns with high expectations, perhaps by saying something along the lines of:

> Honey, I'm sure that in some ways, Dad's home is more fun, and it must be irritating to be expected to do all the chores you do here. I can understand that. The wonderful thing is, down deep, I know that you realize that when you do all the things I ask, it helps you grow to be a helpful and responsible adult. Thanks for your understanding.

Recognize, too, that sometimes the structured parent doesn't provide her child the freedom to explore. The child will have opportunities to choose and learn from mistakes that the other home offers. The important issue is that children learn to recognize that when in Rome, you do as the Romans do: Different expectations occur in different locations, and that's life.

PEARL 14

Eating and Table Manners

Rachel, a loving mom, has spent the better part of her afternoon stooped over a hot stove. She's whipping up a treat, a dish never before seen on the family table: chicken cacciatore. Sweat mingled with seasonings, labor with love.

All eyes were on the proud chef as she carried her covered creation to the dinner table. She lifted the lid, savored the aromatic steam, and then awaited the gasps of appreciation from her loving children. What does Rachel hear instead? A chorus of "Oh, yuck! That stuff is gross!"

"Yuck" can spoil the dinner-table joy, and when dinner-table problems arise—either in displeasure with the food or with tacky table manners—the table becomes less an arena for love than a ground for battle. But not to worry. Rachel's a Love and Logic parent. She was disappointed, yes, but she took the criticism in stride. "No problem," she said as she scooped up her kids' plates and strode to the garbage disposal, where with one flip of the wrist, the problem was resolved.

Then in a soft voice, she said, "Run along, kids. Do what kids do after dinner. We'll see you at breakfast."

Later on that evening, the kids raided the refrigerator. Rachel watched with curiosity, and when her kids had finished eating, she said, "You've just eaten $5.95 worth of food. How do you want to pay me: cash or from your allowance? The choice is yours." The logic behind her words is that she had already bought the food for the evening meal, and kids who rejected that meal and made their own must pay for it.

As with so many things, problems with eating can be eliminated through modeling and choices. Using thinking words instead of fighting words is helpful. Instead of saying, "You eat that, and you eat all of it," or, "I want that plate clean before you leave this table," the Love and Logic parent says, "Have you had enough to make it to the next meal? I hope so, but you decide."

Kids *should* be deciding how much they're going to eat. As they grow older, we won't be in a position to control what they put into their mouths, so the wise parent will ready them for the real world by allowing them to make decisions early.

To introduce new meals, we may want to take a page from Gina's cookbook. Gina never had any problem getting her kids to eat what she wanted them to eat. Her recipe for success: Whenever she cooked anything new and different, she made only enough for two: her and her husband. The kids got hot dogs. Then the two adults lapped up the new dish as if it were the greatest thing ever to come off the top of a stove. "Oh, this is great!" her husband would exclaim. "I hope you cook this more often."

By the end of the meal, the kids would be saying, "Where's ours?" Gina would say, "This is adult food. I don't know if you'd like this." And she wouldn't give them any. The next night, she served the same dish, and she and her husband gobbled it up while raving even louder about how absolutely terrific it tasted. Again, the kids would ask, "Where's ours?" But Gina kept control of the ladle. "It may be too rich for you," she said. "I think kids' taste buds just can't handle this sort of thing. You're probably not old enough."

By the third night, the kids were incensed. "We've got rights!" they demanded. "We want to have some too!" Then Gina relented. "Oh, all right," she said, doling out tiny portions onto their plates. "But don't eat too much." Gina's method encouraged her kids to like what she prepared for dinner.

Dealing with Improper Table Manners

As for table manners, we fall back on the Love and Logic axiom, *If you can't change the behavior, change the location.* Even with the youngest of children, we can nip tacky table behavior in the bud. A one-year-old who spits beets is given a choice: "Eat beets nicely in your chair, or play on the floor." Remember, we are not about punishment or making children feel bad. We are about letting the child know, with love, that when his behavior reaches a certain point (and that will differ with differing parental expectations), the meal is over. If the child feels upset about ending the meal, that's perfectly okay. If the toddler thinks, *Thank goodness—I couldn't stand another minute in that high chair*, that's perfectly okay too!

With older kids, we can vary the technique, allowing them to eat somewhere else—preferably somewhere unappealing—where they can't gross us out with their manners. When Foster's wife, Hermie, was confronted with poor table manners, she dispatched the offending party with one sentence: "Take it to the dryer." Their kids wouldn't gross anybody out but themselves while alone with their plates in the utility room.

Pearl 15

Entitlement

COUNSELOR: "So, Danielle, what's happening in your life that brings you into counseling with me?"

DANIELLE: "It's my parents. They're so lame! All they can do is moan about my credit cards and phone bills. They are so living in the past. They don't get it. There's lots more important things than grades. And they don't have a clue about what kids need. My dad bought me this stupid four-door car. He knows I was supposed to get a convertible. Nobody drives a heap like that to school."

COUNSELOR: "When your dad called to set up these sessions, he told me that money is really tight and that if things don't change, he will have to consider bankruptcy. Given the situation, do you feel any guilt about the amount of money you spend?"

DANIELLE: "Of course not! I didn't ask to be born into this stupid family. Besides, parents are supposed to buy great stuff for their kids."

We're not sure who to feel sorry for in situations like this: Danielle, her parents, or the future of America. As outrageous as Danielle seems, we all know kids like her. We actually feel somewhat sorry for Danielle. Once she started to believe that it is her birthright to have everything she wants as soon as she wants it, she was doomed. She will never have enough to satisfy her. Her happiness will depend upon not what she can attain through effort but how others serve or provide for her. She will enter the adult world expecting far too much from others and far too little from herself.

Danielle's parents tore up their parent license early in her life. By treating her like an honored guest in the home, they became product and service providers instead of parents. As the years went by, they stripped her of the need to act responsibly. As you can tell, she has become more and more dependent on her parents while becoming less and less appreciative of what they provide.

As Danielle enters the adult world, what her parents once provided will become society's responsibility. And as you can guess, that will never be enough to satisfy her. Entitled people see themselves as victims. Once this sets in, all unhappiness and disappointments are the fault of others. Danielle's parents, in their efforts to create a perfect life for their child, failed to teach her that living in a democracy requires personal restraints regarding personal behavior. Her discussion with the counselor indicates that she has no ability to see how her personal behavior impacts others, both in her home and in society.

Many kids arrive at college with wealth they have not earned. They actually have no idea how to attain or maintain their lifestyle other than demanding it from their parents. They have lots of money to spend but no idea how to earn it. In other words, they don't have a clue that the money they spend comes from someone else's hard work, sacrifices, and responsibility. They have pockets full of credit cards without the knowledge of how to use them responsibly.

We have major concerns about the rapid growth of entitlement in our young people and its threat to the American way of life. As we study this problem, we have become aware of the beliefs that entitled people harbor. We like to call these beliefs "The Highs and Lows of Entitlement." As you read, you will become aware that they are all debilitating beliefs:

HIGH: High need for goods and services.
LOW: Low pressure to succeed or hold down jobs.

HIGH: High amount of time to party.
LOW: Low amount of time to devote to accomplishment.

HIGH: High expectations of others.
LOW: Low ambition.

HIGH: High resentment of those who require them to achieve through study and effort.
LOW: Low appreciation for the opportunity for an education.

HIGH: High demand for entertainment and excitement.
LOW: Low awareness of the sacrifices made by their parents.

HIGH: High willingness to defy society's traditional rules and values.
LOW: Low respect for adults and leaders.

HIGH: High inclination to find substitute "highs," such as alcohol and drugs.
LOW: Low respect for society's traditional rules.

These problems and beliefs don't start when kids leave high school. The foundation for these beliefs is created early in life. Actually, this problem is started not by kids but by parents who fail to set reasonable limits for behavior. It is normal for kids to want what they see advertised. However, many parents don't do a good job of helping their kids distinguish between a want and a need. Young children don't naturally place limits on themselves; that is the parents' job.

We often hear parents say, "I don't know what's wrong with kids. They want all this stuff." These parents act as if they don't have a say in the matter. This is not unlike the parents who can't understand that the reason their kids watch too much television is because they allow it. These are the parents who have torn up their parent license. It doesn't have to happen to you. Wise parents do three things:

1. Hold tight to their belief that kids need to learn how to get what they want through their own personal effort and struggle. After all, finding success after such efforts builds positive self-esteem.

2. Develop skills for setting and enforcing limits and boundaries.
3. Surround themselves with like-thinking friends so that they don't have to listen to the mistaken beliefs of those who are busy creating entitled children.

Your Kids Can Be the Fortunate Ones

Obviously, until universities, high schools, community leaders, and particularly parents work together to provide a culture that encourages coping skills by allowing children to experience the fruits of their good and poor decisions, the culture of self-indulgence will be hard to overcome. Thankfully, though, we have seen many parents who are successful at helping their kids avoid the infliction of entitlement. Parents who study and use Love and Logic parenting techniques increase the odds of raising kids who do not show symptoms of entitlement.

Fortunate, indeed, are the children whose parents are willing to let them struggle for, and earn, the goods and services they want.

Fortunate, indeed, are the children whose parents subscribe to the "matching funds" approach. These parents help their children buy goods and services after the kids earn and save a portion of the cost.

Fortunate, indeed, are the children whose parents expect them to do their fair share of the work required to maintain a household.

Fortunate, indeed, are the children whose parents set loving limits, give their children reasonable choices, and allow consequences of those choices to prepare them for the adult world.[8]

Pearl 16

Fears and Monsters

Sometimes they're under the bed. Sometimes just outside the window. Sometimes they lurk under rugs or in closets, ready to spring out in gory horror the moment Mom leaves and extinguishes the last shaft of hallway light. Unless you're a Big Foot believer, you'll agree that monsters lurk in children's heads, and there alone. Every kid, with his or her imagination at full throttle, knows that night creatures don't look like your basic friendly puppy.

One seven-year-old girl, after being adopted, imagined that her new parents only looked like humans but that at night their skin peeled off to reveal their true selves as lizards. As silly as such fears seem to us as adults, they are very real to our kids and may make some hesitate to crack the sheets. But vivid imaginations aside, "monsters" should not keep kids from going to bed.

We must explore children's negative emotions (and their fears of going to bed) in a factual, understanding way without becoming emotionally involved. Simple, calm reassurance that the child is competent to handle his or her own problem helps defuse the child's worry. The situation is not improved when we drop to our knees and personally check under the bed for monsters. Kids are likely to be more afraid, thinking, *Wow! Maybe there* are *monsters. Otherwise, why would she be looking under the bed?*

We can, however, also take advantage of magical thinking. Little kids really do believe in magic. Thus, it's very reassuring for little Benjamin to have a basic "monster-chasing" bear on his shelf. Sometimes only one molecule of Mom's magic perfume on the upper-left corner of the sheet helps Naomi sleep. Such techniques, of course, must be used in a lighthearted, caring way that takes advantage of the way kids naturally think. Furthermore, we should not make too big a deal of such practices. If we don't overly invest in such ploys, they will naturally be discarded as a child matures.

It's worth a few more pennies of electricity to allow night-lights in the hall or bathroom. We can give in on this issue and *not give in* on allowing the child to enter our bedroom to wake us because he or she is afraid. Waking parents up for that reason is a definite no-no.

A discussion to help defuse the monster problem might go like this:

CHILD: "I don't want to go to bed, Mom. I'm afraid I might die tonight."
MOM: "Thankfully, only one child in ten million will die in his sleep tonight, honey."
CHILD: "But I'm afraid."
MOM: "What are you afraid of?"
CHILD: "Monsters."
MOM: "Oh, I wouldn't worry about that. You have Teddy with you."
CHILD: "Can you sprinkle some magic perfume on my covers?"
MOM: "Sure."

Parents who defuse the monster problem by not making a big deal about it or by not encouraging their children's imagination will eventually have kids who go to bed without complaint when they get sleepy.

Pearl 17

Fighting

It never seems to fail. We can buy our sons enough toy trucks to start their own freight line, but when push comes to shove, one specific truck becomes the heart's desire of both boys. They tug and shove and shriek. They won't back down no matter what. It's a maddening phenomenon.

Normal parents who have normal kids have kids who fight. That's one of the things kids do. It's part of growing up. Unfortunately, many of us tell ourselves we're not good parents if our children fight. However, if that were the measure of good parenting, there wouldn't be a single good parent on the face of the earth.

The thing to remember about dealing with our kids' fights is to butt out of them. Expect them to handle their squabbles themselves. This may be the toughest parenting principle to follow because kids desperately want our intervention. In fact, our intervention makes it safe for them to fight. They know we'll step in before anyone gets hurt, so they have no qualms about putting up their dukes.

Our involvement in these spats should involve making sure they occur somewhere far away from us. As soon as the bickering starts to invade our ears, our kids are out of our area with a simple "Hey, guys, take it outside."

Of course we must step in if life and limb are in danger. If a big kid continually terrorizes a little kid—showing relentless anger toward him or her—then we need to stop it. Most of the time, however, we must remember that it takes two to tangle. Even the smallest and frailest of kids has ways to get to big brother or sister. They will submit to hours of punishment simply to watch two minutes of big brother or sister "getting it" from Mom and Dad.

When the tongues have been stilled and fists unclenched, then and only then do we counsel our children about fighting. Trying to reason with kids who are emotionally upset is a waste of good air. Helping our children solve their difficulties involves identifying their feelings. Were they feeling mad, sad, frustrated, left out, or something different? Why did they resort to angry words rather than playing nice? First, they need to identify their feelings, and second, they need to identify different ways of handling them.

We can use modeling at this point: "If I went and hit my boss, Mr. Jackson, whenever I felt frustrated, I probably wouldn't be as happy as if I handled my frustration another way." The point is, we must identify with the child's feelings and then help the child work out a new course of action. However, with really ornery children—ones who glory in brutalizing their peers—it may be necessary to provide them with a significant learning opportunity (SLO).

Foster once counseled a little boy named Kurt who was an expert at terrorizing other little kids. Kurt's *modus operandi* was simple yet effective: He simply aimed for them on the playground and then mowed them down.

Two weeks after Foster placed Kurt in one of his best foster homes, Kurt and his foster mom came in for an appointment. The little lion had become a lamb. He gently held his foster mom's hand. Love bloomed between them. Foster asked, "Kurt, how's the fighting going these days?"

"Oh, I'm not fighting much anymore," Kurt said.

"Well, why not?" he asked. "That was your forte."

Kurt looked up at his mom and said, "Oh, because I hate doing all the chores."

Foster gave the boy a quizzical look. Kurt's rowdy behavior and doing chores didn't seem to connect. Kurt, seeing his perplexed look, explained: "Dr. Cline, when I fight, my mom says it drains energy from the family. But when I clean behind the refrigerator with a hand brush, that puts energy back into the family."

That explained it. In an untrained home, parents would have commanded Kurt to stop his behavior. They would have said, "Kurt, don't you beat up on that other kid or you'll regret it," and Kurt would have had his knees on the other kid's arms before they finished the sentence. But the foster mom had connected Kurt's behavior with a consequence. When Kurt's behavior deteriorated, she could look at him and say, "Kurt, honey, I feel an energy drain coming on," and Kurt would think, *Oh, no, not that!* and there would be no fight.

Pearl 18

Friends

From the time our kids get off the knees of infancy and onto the land legs of toddlerhood, they're going to be around other kids—playing with dolls, shooting baskets, swapping baseball cards, running in the neighborhood. Our kids are going to make friends. That's the good news. As we know, friends are great for kids to have. The bad news is that often we don't like the friends they choose.

One of the biggest mistakes we parents make is getting into a control battle with our kids over who their friends are. We'll lose that one every time. Because we can't win that battle, we should keep our mouths shut and take a different tack. We should concentrate on the areas we can control.

We can offer our kids a choice: Pick friends we approve of and then play with those friends at our house, or pick friends that we don't approve of and then not be allowed to bring them over. Or we can say, "Would you like to have friends who really test your decision-making and thinking skills, or would you rather have some who don't pressure you so much?"

When we try to change our kids' relationships, it may damage our own relationship with our children. Our kids rebel against our demands and orders. Prohibiting our kids from playing with certain friends tells them we are afraid the friends' attitudes, beliefs, or habits will rub off. It also tells our kids that they can't do their own thinking. The result is usually that the friends become more exciting and desirable. But we can tell them what we think. Children cannot rebel against thoughts and opinions. In fact, if our relationship with our kids remains communicative, in the long run our kids will generally pick friends we like.

Tori is about to leave the house to spend time with friends of whom her father doesn't approve.

TORI: "Bye, Dad. I'm leaving."

DAD: "Are you going out with Amber and Melissa?"

TORI: "Yeah, so?"

DAD: "So . . . great! I'm just hoping, dear, that some of you rubs off on them."

TORI: "Oh, Dad."

DAD: "Honey, I'm serious. Sometimes I just think those kids need you around them. Maybe you're a good influence on them or something."

TORI: "You don't like them?"

DAD: "It's not a matter of not liking them, Tori. I just worry sometimes that life may not go as smoothly for those kids as I hope yours goes for you. Have a good time."

We may be pleasantly surprised when we get to know our children's friends. Our kids often see good in others that we simply don't see. When we get to know our kids' friends, we may get to know more about our kids too; we may come to understand why they're attracted to certain people.

Pearl 19

Getting Ready for School

"How many times do I have to call you?"

"You better get yourself moving!"

"You're going to be late for school if you don't step on it!"

How often do we find ourselves barking these commands in the morning? And with good reason, we think. Our morning timetable is tight, the ritual complex. Unfortunately, many times our children move about as fast as the continental drift in their preparations for school. However, the first hour of the day is the very best time to teach kids responsibility. We do this by allowing them to do most of the thinking and most of the jobs we usually do for them. These four general rules will make morning a friendlier time for all:

First, decide which jobs belong to the parents and which belong to the youngsters. A talk with the kids will help them see that setting the alarm, waking up to the alarm, choosing clothes, dressing, washing up, watching the clock, remembering lunch money and school supplies, and even deciding how much to eat are really their responsibilities. The only people to suffer consequences if these are neglected are the youngsters. Our responsibility is to back up the school's consequences for lateness.

Second, stay out of the reminder business. Reminders rob kids of the opportunity to make the mistakes needed to learn lessons.

Third, don't rescue! Rescuing children robs them of the opportunity to learn lessons at emotional times, when the lessons will be best remembered. In other words, if the kids walk to school, no taking them in the car so they won't be late. And no notes excusing their tardiness!

Finally, replace anger with sadness when they make mistakes. Wise parents, when seeing that their kids will be late, say, "Oh, honey, I'm sorry you're going to have a problem with your teacher. I sure hope you work it out."

This dialogue shows how to discuss the getting-up-on-time issue with our kids:

DAD: "What time does the school bus come in the morning, Zach?"
ZACH: "8:20."
DAD: "So, what time do you want to get up?"
ZACH: "Oh, eight."
DAD: "Great. How are you going to get up?"
ZACH: "You'll come and wake me."
DAD: "Well, I always used to do that. But now you're eight years old and most of the kids your age wake themselves up. So how do you think you'll wake yourself up?"
ZACH: "My alarm clock."
DAD: "Good idea. You can set the alarm and get up at eight."
ZACH: "What if I sleep through it?"
DAD: "Well, you'll probably end up being late."
ZACH: "Oh."
DAD: "How will you explain your absence to your teacher?"
ZACH: "That's easy: You can write an excuse for me."
DAD: "I'll be glad to write the truth—that you are having a hard time getting yourself to school and that I will back the school on its punishment."
ZACH: "But if I'm late all the time, they might fail me!"
DAD: "I suppose they might. That would be sad for you."

Chances are, Zach will be up and waiting for the school bus when it rolls around the next morning. Kids with parents who are less concerned about their flunking and more concerned about giving their kids an opportunity to think about flunking develop kids who think and rarely flunk. Their parents aren't going to worry about it, so they'd better.

When Their Tardiness Affects Others

Sometimes our children's morning tardiness affects others too, such as when we must drop them off at school or day care on our way to work. Handling this dilemma takes a little inventiveness.

Five-year-old Jack made his mother late for work regularly. She tried all the standard tactics to get him to be ready: spanking, taking things away, denying television privileges. Nothing worked. Then she decided to give Jack some control. She said, "Jack, I'm so excited. Starting tomorrow, I'm never going to be late for work again because my car will leave every morning at 7:30, and there are two ways for you to go with me. Would you like to hear what they are?"

Jack said, "I guess so."

"Well," Mom said, "dressed is one way and not dressed is the other."

Come morning, Jack (who was not ready to change his behavior that easily) continued his go-slow routine. He wasn't ready at 7:30. Mom came into his room and said, "You're not dressed, but that's no problem. You probably didn't feel like dressing. That's why I have this nice little bag. We'll just put your clothes in here. You can dress whenever you feel like it."

She took Jack by one hand and the bag by another, and out to the car they went. As she backed out of the driveway, she said, "I'm glad I'm going to be to work on time today."

Now, the Jacks of this world are not going to take this lying down. They've got spunk. Jack took his best shot—right at Mom's jugular. "You don't love me," he wailed. "You put me in the backseat of the car with my pajamas still on." Then Jack unveiled the rest of his arsenal. He kicked the back of the seat, squirmed around, and yelled. Soon he was waving to passing motorists like he'd been kidnapped. Eventually, a sad little voice in the backseat was heard: "I guess I'll just have to be dressed on time after this."

It might be necessary, when using this approach, to contact the child's teacher or the day-care superintendent beforehand. Instruct that person not to let the child into the room to participate in activities until the child has his or her clothes on.

Pearl 20

Giving Gifts

What can be more fulfilling than giving our children gifts? But giving a gift provides much more opportunity than simply the fact that a new toy provides our children joy. Most of us stress the importance of teaching our children the *real* meaning of the holidays and how the decorations, tinsel, and gifts are not really what a holiday may signify. But our children's little brains are still often screaming, "What did you get me?" or "What did you bring me?" along with, "Hers is bigger than mine!" or "You got him more!" And the parents often wonder, *Can I get Trey one without getting Jason one too?* Or one parent will say to the other, "Honey, don't you think we've bought the kids enough?"

Many parents rain gifts on their kids. In too many homes, opening gifts is a self-indulgent party in which the child rips the paper off one present, looks at the present briefly, and then goes on a hunting trip for another present to rip open.

There are some Love and Logic guidelines of giving presents that wise parents follow:

Guideline One: If your child shows little appreciation for gifts, give less. If your kid is bored, unappreciative, or not pleasantly responsive when receiving a gift, there is a good chance you are raising an entitled brat. Your child is simply getting and expecting too much.

The old Christmas song warned kids of yore, "Better not pout, better not cry," for Santa checked his list twice for children who were "naughty or nice." Many of today's children believe that pouting and "being naughty or nice" have absolutely nothing to do with the stash they are entitled to receive. They feel they are owed the gifts. If a sincere thank-you is missing, you are raising an entitled child. This is easy to ignore when the kids are younger but often becomes blaming and hostile when they are teens.

Guideline Two: All kids should be equally loved and treated equally. However, equal treatment does not always mean equal gifts.

The happiest parents know (and wise children learn) there are different strokes for different folks. That's the way the world works. Sometimes one kid needs something expensive and the other kid doesn't. Loving parents who generally treat their children equally help their children learn to delay gratification, show appreciation, develop coping skills, handle jealousy, and understand the needs of others when they don't act as if every child needs a gift every time another receives one. Parents who equally love their kids and are equally generous overall don't have to feel like they need to give equal-value gifts on every occasion.

Guideline Three: Don't buy into marketing hype.

By the time the holidays roll around, your kids have been bombarded with advertising pitches. They want a "look-like-me doll" or a particular game. Nothing else will do. It is okay to gratify such whims if the child has knowledge of real reasons the advertised item is attractive. But wise parents help their children to not fall for a pitch: "Wow, they make that plastic rocket look twice as big as it is, and the kids have ten times more fun with it than they really would. I guess you already figured that one out, didn't you?"

It's perfectly okay to say to a child, "Honey, buying stuff like that simply does not fit my value system. It's not what I do. But I can understand your wanting it. You can buy it if you would like!"

Guideline Four: Be creative about opening gifts.

No need to necessarily open all twenty gifts within a twelve-hour period. One family felt it was much more meaningful to the children when the gifts were opened over a period of "the twelve days of Christmas." Let the kids pick which gift they want to open on which day. Then they'll look forward to each gift.

Guideline Five: Teach your child the joy of giving.

The joy of giving more than matches the joy of receiving. Teach your children this. Some of them may not come by it naturally. Show your enthusiasm about giving to others, and it will be contagious: "Wow, I bet when we take this turkey over to the Salvation Army, they will be so happy. I bet this will bring big smiles to their faces!" or "I know it is so hard to pick things out for your brother, but you always seem to light up his life with what you pick. I can hardly wait to be surprised and see what you've chosen this year."

The value of giving gifts is only meaningful if the children spend their own money. This leads most children to be very creative about what they make or buy as gifts. Often a gift that a child makes tends to be more exciting and gratifying than something bought.

Pearl 21

Grades, Underachievement, and Report Cards

"Hailey doesn't understand math very well. We're kind of worried. We talked to her teacher. We spend hours on the problems every night, but we still get Cs and even Ds. And on our first report card, we had a D+. I don't know how we're going to get through the second grade."

Hailey's twin sister talking? Guess again. It's Wendy's *mother.*

This is the cardinal rule for grades and report cards: Parents don't get report cards—kids do. The children sit in class, the children receive the instruction, the children do the work, and the children get the grade. For parents to be effective in dealing with the report card issue, they must keep the monkey on the kids' backs. It is important that children know that the report card is their business. As parents, we care. Our caring might even shade into concern. But solving the problem? That's our children's business.

Foster remembers vividly how his wise dad always kept the report card problem as Foster's responsibility. As a kid in elementary school, Foster had a very difficult time getting started in school. One time he came home with straight Ds. His dad looked over the report card, took out his fat black fountain pen, and paused. "Son, are you proud of this?" he asked.

Foster answered, "No, sir."

"That's good, son." Then his father signed the report card. This ritual occurred time and again. Thank goodness Foster never said he was proud of the report card. He would have had tutoring, private schooling, and heaven knows what all.

The following chart helps us clarify when we should be concerned about our children's performance:

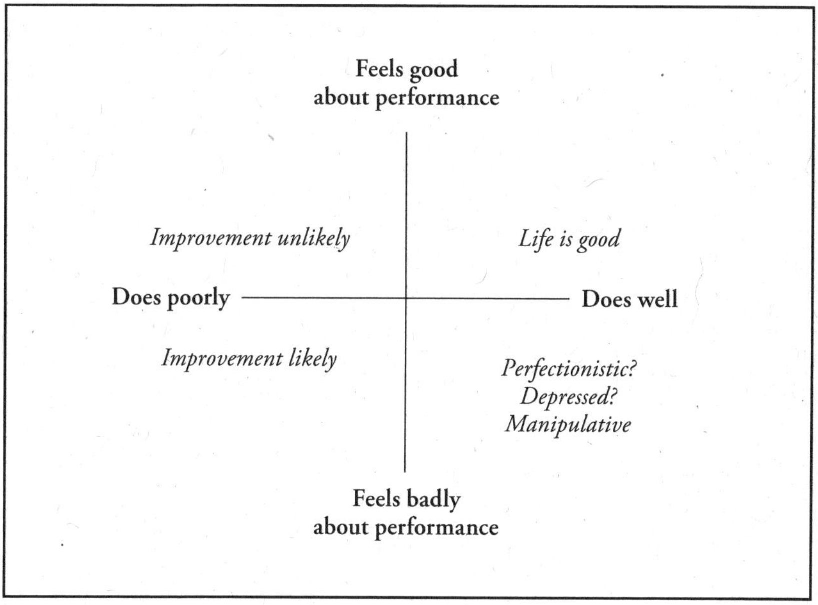

In sum, when kids perform like turkeys but want to become eagles, they eventually fly like pros. But when they perform like turkeys and feel like eagles, they never get off the ground.

With report cards, as with many other issues, children want pizzazz. They want parental emotion. On an unconscious basis, it doesn't matter whether the parental emotion is positive or negative—they'll shoot for it, regardless. Thus, when children return from school offering a report card of mixed quality, parents should enthuse over the positive and be nonemotionally insistent about the negative. A discussion might go like this:

DAD: "Hey, a big A in art! That's great! You always did like art, didn't you?"

CHILD: "Yeah, art is fun."

DAD: "And a B in gym! Well, of course, you always did run like the wind. And another B in music. That's really good! Hmmm, a D in math. Well, I suppose that could be better. Wow, a big B in social studies! It's important to know history and geography. How are you going to handle the math?"

We should always get involved in the areas in which our children excel. If Marissa does well in science, we spend some time together at the pond looking at critters through the microscope. If history turns Griffin's head, we explore books that present it in a colorful and interesting way.

When poor grades are discussed, talk in a nonemotional but caring manner:

- "Do you have any plan for history?"
- "What are your thoughts about the math grade?"
- "Do you think the science grade will get better with time, or will it probably continue to go downhill?"

It is important that the questions do not take on a "witness stand" approach.

In reality, poor grades are not the problem—the *reason* for the poor grades is. Children get poor grades because of poor self-image, rebelliousness to their parents' value system, anxiety, depression, learning problems, and a host of other reasons. Sometimes there is an attitude problem. Some of these reasons may call for a different response. It may be beneficial to have an outsider look at the child's situation and help the parents decide on an appropriate reaction.

Another way of handling this with children is in writing, especially if a dialogue with them is bound to turn explosive. The following is a sample letter a parent could write to the child as a way of responding effectively to this kind of problem. The advantage of putting it in writing is that the youngster has an opportunity to get the parents' complete thoughts before having the opportunity to argue or defend. It usually works best to give the letter with a suggestion that the child think about it for a while before responding.

Dear Son,

Why do I want to know where you are and when you will be home?

Why do I expect you to respect me the way I respect you?

Why do I set expectations for school achievement?

Why do I expect you to do your share of the work around the house?

Why do I expect you to be at family meals?

Why do I set limits for you?

I do these things because it is the best way I know to prove to you that you are important to me and that I love you.

Having expectations for you is not easy. It makes a lot of extra work for me to hold you accountable. You test me frequently to see if I really do love you and believe in you.

You came home late to see what I would do, and you found that I limited your going out for a while. You talked back to me to see if I really loved you, and you ended up giving your sassy words a lot of thought while you were doing some of my chores to make up for the energy drain you caused me. You "forgot" to do your chores and were very surprised when I woke you up that night from a sound sleep to finish the chores. You tested me by being slow getting ready for school and missing the bus. What a long walk that was to school that day. You threw a fit one day at the mall and had to pay for a sitter the next time the rest of us went.

Each time I laid down some consequences for you, it broke my heart. I truly believe that it hurt me as much as it did you. And it was not easy to listen to you tell me that I did what I did because I was mean. Oh, how much easier it would have been to just yell at you or spank you or even excuse your behavior in some way. My love for you and my belief in what you can become was all that gave me strength to do what I needed to do.

I know that many adults who lead happy lives were once children who tested the limits of their parents and did not get their parents to wilt under the pressure. They grew up to be educated and responsible and, therefore, equipped with what they need to have the freedom to achieve their dreams. I also know that the world is filled with people who did not have limits as children. You have seen these people yourself. The only life they will ever live is filled with disappointment.

Yesterday you brought home a report card with grades far below your ability level. Please understand that it would be so much easier for me to make excuses for your behavior than to hold you accountable. It might even make me feel better if I could blame your poor grades on your age, your friends, or even your teacher. But I love you too much to let you down that way.

Please give your school performance some serious thought and be ready to share your plans for solving this problem and getting your academic life back on track. Your father and I will be available to discuss this with you on Friday evening. We want you to be prepared to tell us what you plan to do and also explain to us what kind of support or help you need from us.

I understand that you were hoping to go out Friday evening. Your father and I were planning to do the same. However, we are willing to stay home for this because you are so important to us and we care about the kind of person you become.

In the meantime, we understand you are probably hurting a great deal about your report card. It must be a great disappointment. Please tell your teachers you have our love and support.

Sincerely,
Mom

There are several advantages to approaching the problem in this manner. First of all, it gives both the parents and the child time to cool down and put the situation into proper perspective. It gives the parents time to consult with teachers and counselors. This approach also gives the parents time to rehearse how they want to come across to the youngster when they finally meet on the subject, and it greatly reduces the emotions and power-struggle aspects of the problem. An important factor in dealing with a problem in this manner is that the child gets to learn that the parents' love and support are the most important issues at hand.

Pearl 22

Grandparents

Summertime. Family reunions. Grandpa, Grandma, Mom, Dad, and the kids. Rare and wonderful moments often transpire between grandparents and their grandchildren during these family get-togethers—and between the grown children and their parents as well. Sometimes grandparents care for their grandchildren while the parents are at work. *Grandparenting with Love and Logic* covers intergenerational issues in depth.

Sadly, the parent-child relationship is oftentimes stressed by the behavior of our kids when they're around us and our parents at the same time. Usually kids are fine when alone with one or the other, but put the three generations together and it can be spontaneous combustion. Disagreement occurs when we raise our kids differently than the way we were raised, especially if we were raised with techniques different from Love and Logic parenting.

Grandparents may not understand what is going on between us and our kids. We react to our kids' mistakes with sadness rather than anger; we show kindness rather than protection; we're concerned but not worried. Generally, we give our kids responsibility, allowing for failure and knowing that the price tags of failure are affordable and the children will learn great lessons from their experiences.

In more cases than not, our parents handled us entirely differently. Grandparents who do not understand these techniques may become critical and accusatory: "How could you let that happen to Drew?" they say, and tension within the relationship arises.

Before looking at techniques to avert this tension, we should remember that the model we set with our own parents will be followed by our children as they grow into adulthood. In the way we treat our parents, so too will we be treated by our kids. (Has a shudder run up your spine?)

Also, remember that in a few unhappy cases, parents and children have had a downright toxic relationship. Adult children are sometimes drawn to their parents like moths to a flame—forever being burnt but forever returning, always hoping for a close relationship that will never occur. Clashes over raising the grandchildren are just symptoms of deeper, long-term problems.

Some of us will go through life never being totally accepted or unconditionally loved by our parents, and all the energy spent trying to make it happen will end in only more frustration. This is important to remember as we discuss the four basic rules for parent-grandparent interaction.

Rule One: When we are together with our parents, it must be decided who is going to control the children.

Usually, it should be the parents. If grandparents feel the need to discuss our children's behavior, we should ask them to do so when the child is not misbehaving or present. A good way for them to present their thoughts is, "My relationship with you is really important and I don't want to do anything that stresses it. I have some observations on the grandchildren. Would you like to hear them?" Only if we say yes should the grandparent proceed.

Rule Two: We should be assertive about our wishes.

Rather than reacting to what grandparents say, it is best for us to actively look at the process of how things might be handled. For instance, we might say to our parent, "Mom, before you comment or talk to me about how I raise the children, I hope you will first inquire about it lovingly and ask me why I am handling things the way I do. Does this sound reasonable to you?"

Rule Three: Let the grandparents know why we are with them.

Is it because of a sense of guilt or obligation? Or do we visit because we want to have fun? Sometimes we need to tell our parents, "Mom and

Dad, people get together on vacations either out of a sense of obligation and guilt or to have fun together. I'm wondering if you see our times together as fun. If not, come up with a solution for this, as I'm unwilling for us to relate purely out of a sense of obligation and guilt."

Rule Four: Clarify bottom-line expectations.

It is important that a few things be made clear to both parties. One request we must make of our parents is that they do not comment negatively on our parenting techniques in front of our children. Another might be that they not discipline the kids without our permission. In some cases, it might be necessary to discuss the option of leaving the kids at home so grandparents won't be tempted to meddle.

Likewise, grandparents have rights. If the kids are acting like hellions, grandparents have the right to either ask us to handle it or ask the entire tribe to leave.

If our parenting techniques are decidedly different from those of our folks, it might be wise to explain the principles of Love and Logic parenting before we visit.[9]

In summary, the guidelines for handling grandparents are similar to those for handling children: be assertive, take care of yourself in a healthy way, concentrate on problem solving rather than on frustration and anger, and provide consequences if necessary.

Pearl 23

Homework

Our kids' homework is their problem. It's their pencils that have to move, their minds that must be stretched, and their report cards that have to be brought home. Far too many parents get sucked into the trap that somehow their children's schoolwork is the parents' problem. They hang ultimatums over their kids' heads. They don't let their kids go out and play or watch television until the homework is completed. They deprive and threaten and scream and shout. And if the homework is not done and the grades are not good, they lower the boom.

Our parental responsibility is to provide our kids with the *opportunity* to do their homework. Whether it be for a half hour or an hour or even two hours, our children must sit down at a table or desk with their schoolbooks nearby. That's the opportunity. We allow the kids to choose the place (dining room, kitchen, or their room) and time. We even allow them to choose *whether* to study or not. After all, there are two ways to learn: through actually doing their homework or they can *think about* their homework. Either way, they'll learn—although the lessons will be different. Their teachers at school, who mete out the consequences, might not accept the second way of learning.

Christine effectively handled the homework issue with her son Ian in this way:

CHRISTINE: "Well, Ian, it's time for the homework hour. We've set aside this hour for you to do your homework. Are you ready?"

IAN: "Aw, Mom, do I have to?"

CHRISTINE: "Well, you can learn either by doing your homework or by thinking about your homework. Which do you want to do tonight?"

IAN: "I'll just think about my homework."

CHRISTINE: "You can do it that way if you want, son. I hope you'll be able to get your teacher to go along with it. Do you think he'll accept that method of doing homework?"

IAN: "I don't know."

CHRISTINE: "Well, why don't you give that some thought before you think about your homework tonight. You've got a lot of thinking to do in an hour. So I'll see you when you're done."

There is nothing wrong with parents helping their kids with homework. Many children want help, and we should be there with the needed hint or explanation—but only if our kids ask for it, and only as long as it's profitable. When we start to become irritated, we've helped enough. In this way, we present our children with a positive role model by not allowing *their* problem with homework in an unhealthy way to become *our* problem. But our positive model shouldn't stop there. We show our kids the proper way to approach homework when we talk about the importance of doing our own homework or office work. Saying things like, "I've got to get my homework done," immediately after dinner, or, "I don't feel good doing anything else until I get my work done first," then following through gives our kids an example to imitate.

Unwillingness to do homework is a complicated issue. Laziness is only one cause. A myriad of other underlying causes may be at the core of the problem. The child might have a learning disorder, an attention-deficit disorder, a neurological problem, or an attitude problem. In these cases, treating the symptoms does no good whatsoever. If you determine that these more serious underlying causes may exist, seek professional counseling.

Pearl 24

"I'm Bored" Routine

It's three hours after the dawn of Christmas morning, and calm has replaced flying paper and frantic squeals of delight. Toys, toys, and more toys litter the floor—enough diversion to keep three day-care centers going for years. Then a sad little face emerges from the rubble and a doleful voice is heard: "Mommy, I'm bored." Our inevitable response is, "What? Bored? You've got more toys than all the kids in the Third World put together, and you're bored? No. It's impossible."

Bored kids put the dread in the first day of summer vacation. Continual cries of "Daddy, what can I do?" make us look forward to the day when the big yellow buses resume their daily rounds.

Despite what our kids say, they probably aren't bored. When children say they are bored, it usually means "I want you to spend more time with me." Playing with our kids is one of the great joys of parenting. But when we agree to do so, we should make it plain to them that their boredom is their problem. The parent in the following discussion handled the problem well:

CHILD: "I'm bored. There's nothing going on around here."
PARENT: "Are you really bored? That's too bad. What are your plans?"
CHILD: "Well, what can I do?"
PARENT: "That is a really good question. What kinds of things are in your room?"
CHILD: "Aw, there's nothing in there that I like. I'm tired of it all."

PARENT: "Well, are there things that you like anywhere else in the house?"

CHILD: "I don't think so."

PARENT: "A lot of people get involved with things that they like so they won't be bored. You're saying that when you're bored, there's nothing you really like?"

CHILD: "Right."

PARENT: "So, it looks to me as if there may not be any other option than to sit and be bored. Would you say that was a possibility?"

CHILD: "I guess I could play with my video game."

PARENT: "Would you like me to play one game with you?"

CHILD: "Yeah!"

PARENT: "I guess I could play one game. But if I do that, do you think you'll say, 'Oh, thank you,' or will you whine and say, 'Oh, please, play one more'? How will you handle it if I play only one game with you?"

CHILD: "I promise not to ask for another game."

We want our kids to develop the ability to motivate, interest, and entertain themselves. Allow them to poke their way out of their self-imposed shell of boredom rather than providing them with an entertainment service.

Pearl 25

The Internet

Parents are concerned about the Internet, which, like an apple barrel, is filled with endless worms and rotten apples. At the time of this writing, one-third of all websites contain explicit sexual content. To block that content, parents sometimes use electronic filters. Unfortunately, it is difficult for any filter to adequately screen the thousands of chat rooms that spring up like mushrooms. Pedophiles, identity thieves, and other miscreants are able to troll through chat rooms to strike up conversations with unsuspecting children and encourage them to provide addresses, telephone numbers, and other personal information. By checking the box that affirms that the user is eighteen or over, anyone can access a chat room and sexually explicit material.

It has been estimated that one in five children are solicited online for sex. According to a recent survey, one in five U.S. teenagers who regularly log on to the Internet say they have received unwanted sexual solicitation via the Web.[10] Solicitations were defined as requests to engage in sexual activities or sexual talk or to give personal sexual information.

Love and Logic parents wisely filter their home computers; however, Love and Logic parents wisely don't rely on the filters alone to prevent self-destructive viewing of sexually explicit Internet sites or chats. There are problems with relying on filters:

- Filters have a hard time catching every site.
- Computer-savvy teens may have no problem circumventing filters.

- Unfiltered machines are available somewhere, someplace to all children who seek them out.
- Filters may prevent research on legitimate content. Filters based on keywords may prevent research on breast or prostate cancers.
- Most important, filters say to your child, "You don't have the self-discipline to thoughtfully choose what content to view or how to wisely participate in Internet chats."

Love and Logic emphasizes raising children who control their own behavior. Internet filters are essentially like locking a child in the bedroom because he won't stay on his own. It isn't long before the child says, "You think you can control me from the outside, but you can't control what I do when I'm in here," and then destroys the bedroom, breaks the bedroom door, or climbs out the window.

There is always a way around external control. Even prisons, the strongest of external control programs, experience breakouts. Most external control simply provides resistant and rebellious children with a challenge to circumvent, so Love and Logic places greatest reliance on internal control and on children's self-discipline, which grows as children model loving parents who give factual information.

Children who have the advantage of having Love and Logic parents gradually develop an internal voice that says, *I wonder how my next decision is going to affect me and those around me?* This voice comes from having made bad decisions and living with the consequences while experiencing the love and empathy of their parents. This voice is far more important than all the external controls parents can think up.

So why use filters at all? Filters are a wise first defense but not to be relied upon. Pop-ups, redirects, and malware can surreptitiously display content the user never requested or expected.

The following is an abbreviated conversation between a Love and Logic parent and his son. It shows that before wise parents take any action, they empower their child to be a participant in decision making and the choices that follow:

PARENT: "Derek, what's your take on filtering some of the Internet content on your computer?"

DEREK: "Why? Don't you trust me? I don't need a filter."

PARENT: "It's not a matter of trust. At the office, the business filters content—not because they don't trust us but simply as a way to prevent material that we don't want from sneaking into our computers."

DEREK: "Oh."

PARENT: "There are a number of different types of filters. Some are tighter than others. Some filter all pictures that are sent through e-mail, some are based on sight, and some are based on words. I was thinking we might explore these options together. It's important to me that you feel good about whatever we decide."

DEREK: "Okay."

And here's a conversation a mom might have with her daughter about Internet chat:

MOM: "Honey, you've been doing some chatting on some of the Internet forums, right?"

VANESSA: "Yeah, Mom, it's fun. I've been getting ideas for prom decorations from lots of other kids. There's a whole forum just on prom themes, and it's really fun."

MOM: "And you're talking with other girls about prom stuff?"

VANESSA: "Yeah. I'm so happy I found it. Janelle told me about the site."

MOM: "How do you know you are talking to another girl?"

VANESSA: "What do you mean?"

MOM: "I mean, how do you know you're not talking to a thirty-year-old man pretending to be a teen girl just to get to know you?"

VANESSA: "Well . . ."

MOM: "Sites like the prom site would be the perfect place for a sexual predator to troll around for his next little victim."

VANESSA: "Oh, Mom, you always worry. That won't happen!"

MOM: "Well, it's something to think about." (Mom continues to ask questions—not in a "cross-examine-your-kid" way but with an attitude that reflects curiosity and interest.) "What kind of information do you give the other girls that you get to know?"

VANESSA: "Nothing."

MOM: "Nothing, honey? Not even your school?"

VANESSA: "Well, maybe the school and stuff like that."

MOM: "Do you think that if some sneaky, nasty guy learns what you look like or what you are wearing to a prom that he could identify you on prom night, sort of hang around after that, and nab you?"

VANESSA: "Well . . ."

MOM: "I have some thoughts and observations. Can I share them with you?"

VANESSA: "Sure."

MOM: (setting the model, giving choices) "I'm thinking that if I were you, I'd sleep a lot better at night if I never sent one little bit of information about myself to anyone, and I mean *anyone*, whom I hadn't met face-to-face, because the more dangerous the man, the more he can sound fun, sincere, friendly, caring, and like a great teen."

VANESSA: "Oh . . ."

MOM: "So what's your take on this, honey?"

VANESSA: "You're right, Mom. I'm not going to talk about even my school or anything from now on."

Throughout life, the happiest of people rely on internal controls and self-discipline. The unhappiest of people must rely on external controls to keep their behavior in check. No one sits beside the teen every time he or she drives. Sometime, someplace, somehow, our children must learn to rely on internal checks. Lucky is the child who has parents who encourage this type of learning early on.

Pearl 26

Lying and Dishonesty

Most children, from kindergarten through about the second grade, go through a lying stage. They may be very unskilled with their fibbing, or they may be as clever as the Jim Carrey character in *Liar Liar* before his son's wish, but they're lying all the same.

Dishonesty can turn parents purple with frustration. After all, who wants to raise kids with integrity problems? But we are often at a distinct disadvantage because, frankly, we don't know if they're telling the truth or not! If we catch them in the act, that's one thing. But if we merely suspect fibbing, all of our investigative questioning, done when our kids might be telling the truth, may breed a self-fulfilling prophecy. It's been said that if we wrongly accuse our kids twice for the same thing, they'll set out to prove us right. You can almost hear them say with a sigh, "You think I do it anyway, so I might as well do it." That does not mean, however, that we can't discuss lying with our children. Some healthy doubt is okay.

When talking to our kids about a suspected lie, make sure they're doing the thinking. One effective technique goes like this: "Do you think I believe you right now, or do you think I don't believe you?" If our kids respond with, "But I'm telling the truth," we should resist taking an accusatory tone. Calling children liars is like throwing a grenade at a squad of Green Berets. Kids will fight back—insisting they're telling the truth—simply to protect themselves.

If we think a child is lying, it's better to say, "If it's the truth and I don't believe you, then that's sad for both of us. But if it's a lie and I don't believe you, then it's doubly sad for you." First, the child is telling a lie, and second, he or she is around people who don't believe him or her.

Many parents run scared from saying, "I don't believe you," to their kids. They fear that saying it will somehow destroy their bond of mutual trust. But the phrase is useful. Kids don't have a comeback to it—they can only defend their honesty. We're not calling them liars; we're simply stating that we don't believe them. That makes *them* do the thinking.

However, if we know our child is lying—if we've caught him or her in the act—then the game is over. We say, "Caleb, you *did* hit Bryce in the face. No matter what you say, I saw you do it. Now how are you going to make it right?" The act has occurred; the child is guilty. The only question is, what is the child going to do about it?

Generally, honesty is conveyed to our kids through our actions, not our commands. We need to step back and analyze the model we are presenting to our kids. Do we ever ask our kids to lie for us? Have we ever whispered to our children, "I'm not home," when somebody we don't want to talk to calls on the phone? Do our kids ever see one parent call in sick for the other parent just because Dad or Mom doesn't want to go to work that day? Have we made up lame excuses (translation: *lies*) to get out of social or church obligations? These things may be little, true, but they have more impact on our kids than all the lectures about honesty we could ever deliver.

When kids do tell the truth, Love and Logic parents respond with support. We must say, "Thank you for being honest. I'm sure it was hard for you to tell me that. I bet it was hard on you to know you made that mistake. That is really sad." Then we drop the issue.

Too many parents tell their kids, "It's better for you if you tell the truth," and then they punish their kids for what they did wrong. Such a statement might be true in the long run, but most kids see life through short-run eyes. If they are grounded for a month as punishment for a "crime," it is clearly *not* better for them to tell the truth the next time.

It's best to be more sad for our kids than angry. The consequences will do the teaching, not some unrelated punishment we might impose.

Pearl 27

Nasty Looks and Negative Body Language

"Every time I ask Kate to do something, or even sometimes when I want to talk to her, it happens," one mom said. "She slumps her shoulders and kind of tilts her head a little. Then she gives me a withering look that says, 'Get real, *Mother*.' It really inflames me, and I don't know what to do about it."

Negative body language: those irritating little shows of displeasure our children throw at us whenever we ask them to do something they don't want to do or talk about something they don't want to talk about. The rolling of the eyes, the look of disgust, the stomping off, the slamming of doors—these nonverbal messages say *something*, that much we know. Our question as parents is, *What?*

Most parents believe their children are copping an attitude on them—a bad attitude—but what does Kate really mean when she fires that icy glare at her mom? Is she disappointed, or angry at herself, or trying to say that Mom's unfair, or saying that she feels hurt or let down or criticized? Kate's mom doesn't know for sure, and oftentimes neither do we.

The best response is to say what we have to say, and then walk away. Negative body language is not a problem for us if we don't acknowledge it. But if it continues, we may want to deal with it, and that means thinking of our own behavior. What did we do or say the instant before our child shot his or her eyes toward the sky? Did we criticize our child?

Is he or she merely responding to that criticism? Kids are like adults when it comes to taking criticism: They react to it, often in a negative way. When emotions have cooled and both we and our children are reasonably happy, we can attempt to get at the root of the problem.

MOM: "Hey, Kate, is this a good time to talk?"

KATE: "Yeah, I guess so."

MOM: "I've noticed that sometimes when I say something to you, you give me a certain look, and I have a hard time understanding what that really means. You know, some kids do that because they don't feel it's safe to say that they're hurt or disappointed. Some kids do that because they're unhappy. Other kids do it because they hate their mom and wish she would shut up. Do you have any thoughts on that?"

KATE: "No."

MOM: "Well, why don't you give it some thought? One thing I'm thinking is that maybe I'm doing something to make you feel bad or criticize you or something. If you feel up to telling me something about that, I'd sure be a good listener."

Then Mom should drop the issue and see what happens.

Pouting is another nonverbal sign of displeasure. Kids use it to beg their parents to talk to them. Once we have taken the bait by either asking what is wrong or telling them to get rid of that look, we are doomed. The children now have us as a captive audience. It is often effective to say, "Well, it looks like things are not going well for you right now. When you get yourself to the point of putting your thoughts into words, come and talk to me. I'll be glad to listen." Then break eye contact and move on.

If the negative body language is such a constant that we can successfully predict when it will happen, we might preface our remarks to our child with a comment like, "Hey, Kate, I have something I want to share with you. Now, when I get through, you may want to melt me with that laser look you're so good at, so get it ready." It's hard for kids to do something we have given them permission to do; they don't feel as if they're in control.

When we consider the range of options open to our kids when they're unhappy with us—everything from ignoring us to telling us where to go—the rolling eyes or the steely gaze aren't so bad. It gives our kids the chance to save face and retain some control. We all need that opportunity when placed in a situation we're not pleased with.

Pearl 28

Pacifiers

In our lives, we have seen many ideas come and go: constant cigarette smoking in public places, collecting pet rocks, and the fad of birthing children into a pan of warm water. What do all of these have in common? Through the course of history, many normal human beings didn't engage in these behaviors. One might say that the behaviors simply aren't "normal" responses of the human race. Use of a pacifier in toddlerhood falls into this category.

In the past, did children walk around with a nipple in their mouth? No more than adults walked around with a lit weed and smoke coming out their nose! During the early critical times of brain development, pacifiers lock in neural connections that essentially tell a child, "Get frustrated, get bored, get fussy—and handle it by putting something in your mouth."

Throughout history, infants may have had a nipple in their mouth much of the time. But *toddlers*? No. No mother of yore provided a nipple manufactured or otherwise for her child to put in his mouth and walk around. The child had to at least be creative enough to decide for himself what he might want to suck on.

Pacifiers tend to be isolating in toddlerhood. Even the mothers who earlier encouraged their children to suck on a pacifier have a bit of uneasiness when their child walks around with a pacifier in his mouth. And strangers—particularly men—almost never think a toddler walking about with a pacifier is "cute." In fact, such a child is approached *much* less than a child who looks at a person and smiles without a pacifier.

Many adults immediately look another direction.

Once a child gets used to a pacifier, it becomes almost an addiction. The child wants that pacifier like an alcoholic wants the bottle—and, on a neurobiological level, both responses may be related.

Children, if they need it, can generally find something to suck on. One of Foster's daughters carried around a favorite rabbit and sucked on its ears. The problem was solved by progressively clipping the rabbit's moldy ears shorter and shorter. Everyone was excited! "Look at that, honey, all gone! The rabbit has molted its ears!"

Many parents have a difficult time encouraging their child to outright *quit* sucking on something, but almost all parents can succeed when they concentrate on *where* the sucking happens. This is much more effective:

> "Honey, it looks as if you are into sucking your pacifier right now, and I'm sure it feels super-good to you, but it is a hassle to my eyeballs, so I will appreciate it if you practice it up in your room. When you get it out of your system, will you join us again?"

Toddlers soon learn that when they behave in a way that hassles others, they will be asked politely, with consideration and *without* parental frustration, to leave the area for a given length of time.

Pearl 29

Peer Pressure

The battle over peer pressure begins when our children are two or three years old. That doesn't mean our diaper-clad youngster will toddle through the door tomorrow with a purple Mohawk hairdo and a nail-studded motorcycle jacket. Kids are growing up quicker than ever before, but not *that* quick. It does mean that the battle of the dominant voices in each child's head starts in toddlerhood. Isn't that what peer pressure is all about—kids listening to the voices of their peers rather than thinking for themselves?

Many of us unwittingly train our children to listen to their peers by teaching them, while young, to listen to a very strong voice outside their own head: *ours*. We say, "Do what I tell you to do, do it now, and do it my way." When these children hit adolescence, a very profound shift in their thinking occurs. They say, *I can now think for myself. I don't have to listen to that strong voice outside my head.* So they begin to think for themselves, right? Wrong. Consider their quandary. They've been conditioned for about eleven years to listen to our voice. They're not going to listen to us anymore (they've decided that), and they can't listen to a voice inside of their own heads (there isn't any; we've done all their thinking for them up to that point in their lives). So the only voice that registers is that of their peers—another voice coming from outside their heads.

Many of us throw up our hands in frustration when our children hit eleven or twelve years of age. We might say, "My kids used to listen to me, but now they won't. Boy, have they ever changed." Wrong again.

They haven't changed one iota. They're still listening to a voice outside their heads—it's just not ours anymore.

The first step in preparing our children to cope with the peer pressure they'll meet down the road is to start them early in listening to that small voice inside their own head. Give them choices on little things: Chocolate or white milk? The blue coat or the red coat? Put the mittens in the pocket or wear them? They have to decide; the little voice inside their head does the talking.

The more decisions kids make, the more times we ask them questions instead of telling them what to do, and the more we discuss issues using thinking words, the less likely they'll be negatively influenced by peers later on.

We shouldn't fool ourselves, however. Peer pressure will still be strong. During those early preadolescent and adolescent years, our kids are trying so hard to build social skills, and friendships will be crucial. But with good preparation, their own inner voice will have a fighting chance.

Second, when our children hit eleven or twelve, to prepare them to cope with peer pressure, it is essential we have little discussions with them from time to time about the pressures of adolescent life. For example:

DAD: "Miranda, I know how hard it is to be facing adolescence now and how important your friendships are to you. Mom and I want to support you in your friendships and everything else you may be going through. I just want to have a little talk today to see how that's going for you and whether or not you're able to think when you're around your friends. Okay?"

MIRANDA: "Uh, okay, I guess."

DAD: "I thought maybe we could talk about your plan for making sure you get to be yourself, because I know you're working very hard not to be your parents. So the next job is to learn how not to be your friends, too, and instead become yourself."

Another fruitful area of discussion involves the concept of saying no. Will our children be able to say no to their friends? If we have allowed the voice inside their head to gain in volume and quality over the years, they will. But we should teach our kids to say no to their peers in the same manner we say no to them: by saying yes to something else. If friends want them to try drugs (this can happen before they hit their teens, by the way), it's easier for them to decline the offer by saying, "Hey, I'd be glad to go roller-skating, or to the mall, or to the yogurt shop. I want to do something with you, but I'd like it to be something other than drugs." Kids feel a lot stronger when they know how to say yes to something else rather than just saying no and feeling out of it and alone.

It also helps if we offer ourselves as fall guys. We should tell our children, "If you need to say no to a peer and you want to use us as the bad guys, feel free to say, 'No, my folks would kill me if I did that!'" This is one additional tool we can give our kids.

Pearl 30

Pet Care

Our pets are there when we need them, providing companionship and love. And they're consistent—they seem to always be *up* (except for cats—who can figure them out?).

Pets provide our kids with a wonderful opportunity to learn responsibility. Most of us agree to take pets into our homes with the proviso that they are our kids' responsibility. Our kids must feed them, clean their messes, and tend to their houses, cages, or tanks. But all too often, we end up trudging along behind Fifi with the pooper-scooper or transferring Goldie and Hawn into a mixing bowl so we can scrub the rocks in their fish tank.

It doesn't have to be like that. We can keep the responsibility of pet care on our children's shoulders, but it takes real parental *chutzpah.*

One mother of two girls lived by the mealtime motto "I feed only four mouths." If her daughters hadn't fed the family's cat and dog by 5:00 p.m., then the four mouths were Mom, Dad, cat, and dog. "You're not eating dinner tonight," Mom would explain to her daughters, "because I used my energy feeding Fred and Charlemagne instead." Then she would give her daughters a kiss on the cheek, smile, and say, "We're sure going to miss you at the dinner table."

If that technique doesn't get results, then wise parents will attempt to find the pet a different owner. Explain kindly and without criticism to the children, "Buster really needs somebody who will feed him on a regular schedule," or, "Budgee needs someone who will always clean the cage because he really must have his cage cleaned." Then give the animal away.

Another point of view that is acceptable to the authors of Love and Logic is that parents take care of the pets, and the kids take care of the parents by doing adult chores to replace the time and energy expended by the parents.

The other alternative is to take care of the pets ourselves. But if our children know that Smokey will be fed by Mom or that Rodent's cedar chips will be changed by Dad, they'll cease to worry about Smokey or Rodent. Pet care is then our problem, not theirs. The choice is ours.

PEARL 31

Picking Up Belongings

The unofficial world record for trashing a living room was set in early 1987 by a Colorado lad named Bobby. In forty-five seconds, this five-year-old tornado could bounce seventeen teddy bears down two flights of stairs and scatter three cylinders of Lincoln Logs, two complete sets of Legos, four boxes of Crayola 64s, and enough plastic army men to invade the next county. By the time he'd dumped his big sister's 500-piece puzzles, you couldn't even see the carpet. *Not a bad minute's work,* Bobby would say to himself as he surveyed his handiwork, *but it's sure too messy in here to play. I'm going down to the basement.*

Kids and their toys. We can be sitting in relative order one minute, but let kids loose with their belongings, and before we can turn a page in the evening paper, the room is trashed. Who usually cleans it up? Us. It's a double whammy. We have to do the work, plus our children don't learn how to care for their belongings.

Modeling is the secret to instilling a sense of responsibility about personal belongings. Our kids will do as we do. Unfortunately, some parents can't blame their kids for not picking up their toys. Mounds of clothes drape the chairs of the master bedroom, and it took two hours to find the mower in the garage the last time the lawn needed a trim. These parents don't take care of their own belongings. As kids enter the stage in their lives when they want to be big and feel big, they imitate the big people in their lives—their parents.

In addition to using actions to model, we can also talk to ourselves or to our spouse in order to get the point across. For instance, talking about how good we feel when we know our things are neatly put away tells our kids it's great to be neat. Putting the dishes away, returning the tools to their proper hooks, sweeping the sidewalks after mowing the grass—if we're talking about it as we do it and after we do it, our kids get the right message.

Until our kids hit kindergarten, cleaning up their toys should be a community project. We put away a toy, then they put away a toy, then we put away a toy, and so on. After that age, however, their toys are their responsibility. What happens to them is up to the kids. If they leave them lying around their room, that's one thing. We don't make a big issue out of it. But if every time we take a step across the family room we stub our toes on a toy truck, that's another. One parent handled the issue like this:

PARENT: "Hey, Kyle, there's a lot of your stuff lying around the house today. It's kind of getting in the way. Do you want to pick it up, or would you rather I picked it up?"

KYLE: "You pick it up."

PARENT: "Well, the advantage of your picking it up is that you'll get to see it again. If I pick up, I'll keep the stuff. So you might want to rethink your decision on that. But you don't have to rush. I'll know what you want. If by lunchtime I still see your stuff out there, I'll know you decided to have me pick it up. If I see that it's gone, then I'll know that you decided to pick it up for yourself."

If we end up moving the toys, the question then becomes, *Should we give them back to our child?* That depends on how responsible the child generally is. If our child is basically responsible, then we'd say, "No problem. Every time you pick up all of your things by yourself without being told, you earn back one of the toys you lost today." But kids who have a hard-core problem with responsibility should know they are gradually saying bye-bye to the toys we have to pick up. But don't feel too bad about it. In most American homes, kids have far more toys than they need or know how to take care of.

Also, don't be afraid of saying from time to time, "I'm really worried about the way you're taking care of your model car. I'm thinking maybe you need to be a little older before you have that responsibility. So I'm going to take that toy until I don't have to worry about how well you're taking care of it. You'll get another shot at it sometime. But don't worry about it—there's no big hurry." There's no hurry for us, that is. We aren't going to worry about that toy. But the children will, and that translates into an attempt on their part to be more responsible.

Pearl 32

Professional Help: When to Seek It

A delicate question often arises from parents of troublesome children: "When should we seek professional help?" First, get it out of your head that seeking professional help is an admission of failure. In our complex society, with its myriad social problems, our kids quite naturally face dilemmas we never had to cope with during our childhood. Societal pressures for success, for example, are overwhelming, filtering down even to the lower grades. Peer pressure prompts kids to insist on the latest designer jeans and the coolest brand-name sneakers—when they're still in kindergarten! More kids than ever before have severe problems, and the causes of those problems stand apart from the method or intent of parental discipline.

Thus, we offer two guidelines for seeking professional help:

1. If you have read this book—taking in the Love and Logic philosophy and applying it consistently to your children—and you still have big problems, then you need professional help.
2. If a situation has gotten progressively worse over a three-month period and no improvement is in sight, you should seek out a counselor.

Professional care does not necessarily mean a long, drawn-out series of counseling sessions. Oftentimes, one session with a trained counselor who knows what he or she is talking about is enough to straighten out the problem.

Pearl 33

The Room: Keeping It Clean

The eyes swivel furtively down the hall. No footsteps. No voices. It *seems* safe. The hand creeps slowly, tentatively, to the doorknob despite the ominous warnings posted all around: "No Trespassing," "Keep Out," "Enter at Your Own Risk."

Sometimes a mom must risk personal safety in pursuit of a greater cause—even if that cause is nothing more than curiosity. She turns the knob and waits. Nothing. No booby traps. No sirens. No Teenage Mutant Ninja Turtles lunging to grab her throat. A welcome breath of relief passes her lips. Carefully, cautiously, she pushes open the door, shielding her eyes in preparation for the sight. But it is too much. She screams.

Entering a child's room can be hazardous to your health. The condition of that room—or the toxicity of the health hazard, as the case may be—can be cause for a great deal of parent-child friction. How much effort to expend on the "condition of the sty" really depends on the age and responsibility level of the child.

Toddlers and preschoolers can be taught the joy of having a clean room by parental example. Parents can join the child in cleaning the room, talking all the while: "Doesn't it feel good to get all twenty-five of your stuffed Snoopys in a row?" or "I feel so much better now that I know you won't trip on those dust balls."

When we help our tykes clean their room, the unspoken message we send is that there's the job, there's fun, and there's us helping them. However, when our children hit the third grade, it's time to take one large step back and out of the picture. Then there's the job and there's fun but no *us*. We relinquish control and allow our kids' room to be their own private domain.

A child's room is a great learning ground for an irresponsible kid. If our kids are not at the level of responsibility they should be, we can take the large step back into the picture.

The state of our kids' room is a control battle we can win. But making an issue of it doesn't mean yelling at them. It means offering choices and using other Love and Logic techniques. Here again we want to avoid telling our kids when to clean their room. Much better is to set a certain time by which they must have it done. A conversation might go like this:

PARENT: "Would it be reasonable for you to have your room cleaned by Saturday morning?"

CHILD: "Aw, I don't want to clean my room."

PARENT: "Well, that's okay. You don't have to. You can hire me or your sister or your brother to do it. We'd love some extra cash."

CHILD: "But I don't have any money."

PARENT: "You know, when adults don't have any money, they sell something."

CHILD: "Sell something?"

PARENT: "You don't have to decide now what you're going to sell. You can tell me by Saturday. If you can decide by Saturday, that means you get to choose what to sell. And if you can't, that means I choose. So you have a choice of who chooses. That's up to you."

Chances are that child will decide to clean his or her room.

In summary, when children are small, having fun cleaning the room together with a parent helps teach the joy of responsibility. As they get older, have more activities, and collect more stuff, their room is no cleaner than our hotel room after a week's vacation. There's just not enough room, and there are other things to do. Kids keep their room about as clean as we keep the garage—and for the same reason. It's a storage area.

Pearl 34

The Room: Keeping the Kid in It

The relationship between kids and their room is a curious thing. As parents of teenagers know, sometimes the hardest thing in the world is to get them out of their room. For them it is a secret, private place, far removed from the turmoil of adolescent life. But when kids are little, the problem is different: They won't *stay* in their room.

Kim summed up her problem with little Noah: "When Noah is a nuisance to my ears, I follow the Love and Logic plan. I decide what's best for both of us. And if I can't change his behavior, I change the location. I pick him up and haul him to his room. But as soon as I set him down and walk down the stairs, there he is, following me."

Once we've sent our kids to their room, how do we make them stay there? Kim did one thing that we should avoid: physically carrying the child to his or her room. Except when our kids are very small, when we can put them in a crib, they should go to their room under their own power.

When the child is around age two, a statement—"I want you to go to your room, and I want you to go now"—spoken firmly and with index finger pointing toward the room will usually get results. If the child toddles back out, we should offer, "Would you like to stay in your room with the door open or shut?" If this fails, we can follow with, "Would you like to stay in your room with the door unlocked or locked?" Then, if we are forced to lock the door to keep him in, we need to stay right by it and, once the child has calmed down, open it to again offer him a chance to stay in the room with the door unlocked for five more minutes to practice the appropriate behavior. An egg timer is a great aid for this. When the timer dings, give him a hug for his accomplishment and let him play near you again.

Sometimes kids want to leave their room because of some previous traumatizing experience, such as hospitalization or surgery. These children need our special understanding, and often a good discussion with much reassurance helps them overcome their fears. But knowing the reason for the problem is not an excuse to let it continue. If the behavior persists, we must allow them to work it out.

In addition to disciplinary situations, another major problem parents face is when children frequently wander out of their room at night, waking their parents for drinks of water or because they're afraid. A night-light may help cure this problem. If the child continues to pester parents at night (many kids will), a more direct solution is needed.

Set up an evening or two to deal with the problem. On that evening, say to your spouse, within the child's hearing, "We need to get a good night's sleep, and that's difficult to do with Tanner around. How about you and me going to the Holiday Inn tonight? We'll be able to relax and get a good night's sleep." Then the parents would give Tanner a loving kiss and hug and call a babysitter, whom they've notified earlier, to come stay with the youngster overnight.

The babysitter has a role to play too. He or she should say things to the child like, "Looks like your parents need a good night's sleep. Maybe they need only one night, but they might need more." If the child wakes the babysitter in the middle of the night, he or she should be nonresponsive: "I don't know what to do with kids who get up in the middle of the night because I don't have any kids who do that." The babysitter may have to do this two or three times during the night, but it's absolutely important that he or she not give in to the child's request.

There should be no anger on the babysitter's part or yours. We blow it completely when we say, "Just see how you like spending the night without us in the house. How are you going to feel about that?" The child then becomes angry at us instead of concerned about his or her own problem. Phrases like "We have to leave the house," "You're making us leave," or "Look what you're making us do" also send the wrong message.

We leave the house for one reason only: We want to get a good night's sleep. Say something like this: "Honey, we need a good night's sleep, and we might have to leave home tonight to do that. We might want to do this a lot of other nights because it's really good for Daddy and me to get a good night's sleep. Sometimes we sleep better when we're away from you."

Many kids who get up in the middle of the night are dependent on their parents. Sometimes the only way to cure this dependence is to not be there for them. This may seem like an extreme, complicated, and expensive solution, but if you're a parent who has not had a decent night's sleep for months or years, this approach is well worth the effort and cost. You can even do it for free if friends with a similar problem want to trade houses for a night. Kids are reluctant to bug "strange parents"; they don't know which buttons to push.

Pearl 35

Sassing and Disrespect

"I don't have to listen to you, so shut up!" If you've ever been downwind of an explosion of defiant words like these from your child's mouth, you probably know all about your reaction. Purple face. Clenched fists. Pursed lips. Temptation to sprint for the paddle. And all of that is just a prelude to the fireworks that follow.

Disrespectful kids are tough to take. They seem to have a smart-aleck comeback for everything we say. The trouble is that when we detonate a fireworks display in response, we are actually rewarding our kids for sassing us. We are giving our children emotion. And kids thrive on parental emotion; they lean back and enjoy the show. It's part of human nature. Sermons on fire and brimstone usually will outdraw those concentrating on Jesus' love. Humankind doesn't want peace; it wants emotion.

Rather than saying, "No child of mine is going to speak to me like that," followed by a sermon-length lecture on respect, Love and Logic parents make it clear from the start that sassing does not result in an emotional response.

The key to defusing sassy kids is to get them out of our sight and earshot until they can speak quietly and calmly and our blood pressure has dropped fifty points. But we don't dictate their exile. We let them pick the banishment of their choice: "Would you like to go to your room or down to the basement? Come back when you can talk as calmly as I'm talking right now."

Observe how Suzanne handles her disrespectful son Calvin:

CALVIN: "I don't have to listen to you. Shut up!"

SUZANNE: "You know, Calvin, no one can make you listen. And I think right now we're having a hard time listening to each other. So why don't you go someplace else for a while?"

CALVIN: "I don't have to go someplace else. This is my house, too, you know. I live here. Besides, you never listen to me."

SUZANNE: "Calvin, I'll be glad to listen when you've calmed down. But I think you'd be a lot happier if you went someplace else for now."

CALVIN: "You never listen to a word I say!"

SUZANNE: "I think you'd be a lot happier if you went someplace else."

CALVIN: "It's not fair!"

SUZANNE: "Sorry you see it that way, but I think you'd be a lot happier if you went someplace else."

With sassy kids, use the broken-record routine. Getting them away from you until calmness sets in is the primary mission. But don't forget that discussion you promised. When tempers have cooled and words can be spoken without a flush of color coming to anybody's face, try to discover the child's reason for being disrespectful.

At that point, it is useful to say, "I notice that you often have words for me when I ask you to do things. I wonder if I'm hearing it the same way you mean it. I'm confused about what you're trying to tell me. Are you trying to tell me that you're embarrassed, or that you feel put down, or that you want to be the boss, or that you hate me, or that you just don't know a better way to answer, or what?" This usually leads to a discussion. It is absolutely essential that you listen without being defensive or judgmental. (Be ready to part ways again if you feel the emotions rising.) After the discussion, say, "Thanks for sharing." This will keep them thinking about their response rather than yours and help them find better words for disagreements in the future.

Pearl 36

Spanking

"Daddy, why can't we just have a spanking and get this over with?"

Six-year-old Olivia had just slipped quietly into the living room, where Dad was reading his paper. She begged, "Our friends get to have spankings, and then they get to play. If you give us a spanking, we'll never play in the street again. We're tired of waiting for you to decide what you're going to do."

Yeah, thought Dad. *Spankings are a lot easier than having to wait and think about what you've done wrong. They give kids a quick escape from the responsibility of living with a bad choice. Instead of having to live with consequences and think about solutions, youngsters have a brief moment of pain, and then they're off the hook.*

The original edition of this book advocated the use of spanking in limited, controlled situations. However, as we have grown in our professions and as more valid research has become available, we have changed our position.

There are many good reasons to avoid the use of spankings:

- Empathy and logical consequences are far more powerful than spanking because they teach problem-solving skills.
- Spanking fails to teach the behaviors we want kids to emulate later in life.
- Most kids would rather receive a spanking than have to think about their poor choice.

- More recent research tells us that spanking has many negative side effects, such as anger, resentment, and the desire for revenge.
- Our kids may someday choose our nursing homes.

Love and Logic techniques often leave children wishing for spankings. We were first introduced to this idea when a student from Jim's school, where Jim was the principal, spilled the beans to his therapist. This wonderful counselor, using some reverse psychology, asked this boy, "Tony, do you *really* have to do what those teachers tell you? Maybe you can get by without following the school rules."

"Oh, no! Oh, no!" yelled Tony. "You have to do what they tell you! If you don't, you have to go to Mr. Fay's office and think! I'm not going through that again—no way!"

Unlike the previous principal, Jim refrained from using the paddle. The simple rule in his office was that kids had to solve the problems they created. They were constantly asking him for spankings instead.

Pearl 37

Sports

As parents, most of us want our kids involved in sports from the time they are very young for a number of reasons: the exercise, socialization, character-building, learning to be a team player, sportsmanship, and so on. Because of this, it is not uncommon to see toddlers out battling over a soccer ball or whacking a baseball off a tee before they even understand what game they are playing.

Recent studies have also shown that our kids today have half the unstructured play time kids did only a generation ago, because we are running between school, dance, baseball, basketball, or other practice and parents don't feel as comfortable as they once did about letting little Jimmy or Sharon walk down the street to play at a friend's house more than a block or two away. Families also eat dinner together a third less than they used to.[11] These facts have led to the age of the soccer mom and coach dad we live in today, and kids who rarely get out of the house unless it is for some planned event, which is generally sports-related.

Another issue that has evolved from this shift in how we spend our time is the fact that sports have always battled between two philosophies: (1) *It's not whether you win or lose, but how you play the game*; and (2) *Winning isn't everything—it is the only thing.* Throw in with that the dream of many parents that their kids will someday play in the big leagues (even though less than 5 percent of our kids will go on to do so) and this cultural shift has created some incredible new pressures on our kids—pressures that, in the end, have many of our kids dropping out of sports before they reach high school age.

In our opinion, kids' participation in organized sports is a great thing as long as the focus stays primarily on the positives—character-building, working together, staying fit, and so forth—and only secondarily on the competition and drive to "be the best." Playing sports provides a wonderful arena for kids to try difficult things and gain self-confidence from mastering new skills. While it is great that parents encourage their kids to participate, ultimately it has to be the kids who want to play because they enjoy the game and not because their parents want them to be a team star. With sports as with other issues, Love and Logic ultimately wants the kids to choose, not the parents.

A father wrote to us recently relating his experience with his son, Love and Logic, and sports:

> My son and I often had conflicts over his performance on the sporting field. Since he was young, he has always played soccer, and I have coached his baseball team the past three years. Last winter, for a number of reasons, he decided to drop out of basketball because 'it just wasn't his game,' and he wanted to focus more on his other two sports. This was hard on me, growing up in a time when everybody playing three sports was the norm, but it seems times have changed, so I agreed to help him work more on his baseball and soccer skills.
>
> Last year was especially hard. As his soccer league had grown more competitive, he was playing less and less over the year. We had numerous conflicts about his coach, his effort, and whether or not he would continue the sport. I was also trying to coach him on the way home from games and he wanted to hear less and less of it. I felt a rift growing between us and I didn't know what to do about it. I wouldn't let him quit, but I also knew that if he didn't want to play, it didn't matter what I thought, I couldn't *make* him try harder—he had to want to.
>
> With the beginning of this new school year and fresh soccer season, things seemed better. He had a coach who was playing him more and he was performing better on the field. Then a couple of weeks ago, he had a game where he just seemed dead on the field, and all the old frustrations came back about his

efforts and his attitudes. I was so upset as the game finished, I was ready to lay into him with a Vince Lombardi halftime speech about winners and losers.

However, having read *Parenting with Love and Logic* recently, I knew that now that he was eleven, he had to choose to play the game or else he would soon quit—I couldn't make him play harder. So I decided to do the difficult thing—I kept my mouth shut to let him talk about the game.

As we walked back to the car I was fuming and had to excuse myself to stop at the restrooms to calm down before we drove home. The car was silent on the way home, and I refused to let him turn on the radio to give him time to think. When we arrived home, we discovered he had left one of the sandals he wears before and after the game at the field, so we drove back. That was also a quiet ride until about halfway back when he asked me, 'Why did you yell at me to go when that kid fell down?' While he was fighting for the ball with another boy, the kid had fallen to the turf and the whole sideline yelled for him to take the ball and go toward the goal. I explained to him that I didn't see that the other boy was hurt, but that, if he had been concerned, the correct thing to do was kick the ball out of bounds so that the official could call time out to allow the coach to come and check on him. Then I apologized for getting so excited.

After that, the layers of the onion began to peel as his focus changed from outside—my yelling on the sideline—to inside—how he felt about his performance and how badly he had wanted to play well in front of his mom, whose schedule didn't allow her to come to very many of his games. He talked of how he wanted to show her that he was playing because he liked the game and not just because I wanted him to play. Again, I just let him talk, but my emotions had changed from being mad to being proud of him—and even a little choked up.

We finally arrived back at the field and found his sandal, and then I decided to go get some smoothies so we could continue our discussion. Over the smoothies we discussed his performance a bit more, why he had felt sluggish (too much water before the game), and he even listened as I gave him a couple of pointers on what he could do to address some of the problems he felt he had had on the field that day. It was one of the best times I have ever had talking with him.

Since then, I have let him own his sports more, and he has even asked me to go out and play catch with him a couple of times so that he can get ready for baseball season, which is his true love. The old image of a dad playing catch with his son has lost none of its nostalgia.

Letting him own his sporting efforts and not taking them away from him by getting too emotional and telling him how to play the game has made all the difference in the world.

Pearl 38

Stealing

Of all the problems that surface with our kids, nothing affects our emotions quite as much as their stealing. The right of property holds a high place in our moral hierarchy. We want our kids to respect what is theirs and keep their hands off what isn't. But some children do steal. Usually our kids' stealing cannot be cured by a direct frontal assault on the stealing itself. Instead, it has to be handled by understanding and reckoning with the underlying feelings that led to the act in the first place.

Fortunately, as with lying, early stealing—that is, between the ages of four and six—is almost always simply a childhood phase. If we handle it matter-of-factly, without too much anger, invariably most children quickly outgrow the stealing phase. An emotional response from us, however, usually makes matters worse because kids get defensive and fight for control. Let's look at the two approaches in action.

Four-year-old Sophie lifts an earring from her mom's jewelry box. Mom finds out and shrieks, "Sophie, did you take this earring? Don't just look at me—answer me! I told you not to get into my jewelry box. This really makes me mad. You put it back right now, and don't you *ever* do that again!" Without realizing it, by vibrating so much emotion, this mom is teaching Sophie to continue her stealing. The child will start going out of her way to upset Mom. Stealing becomes kind of exciting for Sophie—a lot of noise and no consequences.

A better way of handling the incident would have been for the mom to say, "Sophie, honey, Mommy doesn't like it when you take her earring. Now take it back to the box. Thank you. Oh, thank you for putting it back! That makes Mommy so happy. What a good girl." By approaching it this way, Mom gives Sophie good feelings for making sure the earring is put into the right place, not emotion because the earring was taken in the first place.

Chronic stealing, however, can be a different story. A parent-child control battle may be the cause, or the problem's roots may run deeper. Stealing almost always occurs when a child is feeling empty or unloved. The child's feeling of emptiness can come on suddenly, or it can be long term. The child may steal in much the same way that people bite their fingernails: by habit. Inside, these kids are saying, "I'm not getting my fair share. I should have more."

With chronic stealing it is important for us to get at the underlying issue, whether it is the child's poor self-concept or his or her feeling of being "unfaired upon." Talking with our children (when the problem is not occurring), building their self-concept, and demonstrating our love for them will help tremendously.

Stealing is a multifaceted problem that usually cannot be dealt with directly, but children's feelings of loss, emptiness, or being treated unfairly can be addressed with understanding, touch, eye contact, hugs, and the use of sensible consequences.

Pearl 39

Swearing and Bad Language

It hits us like an ice-water Jacuzzi. That innocent little foundling we once dandled on our knees and whose vocabulary consisted exclusively of coos and goo-goos tramps through the door one day spewing forth a string of expletives that would make a dockworker blush. Sometimes our kids are mimicking their schoolmates. Other times they seem to use obscenities merely to watch our neck hairs stand straight out. Whatever the reason, our children's bad language can be a troubling thing for us.

In many cases it is a mere rite of passage—a phase kids go through on their journey to maturity. They hear older kids swearing, and wanting to be big like them, they develop a vocabulary more in tune with that used under an NBA backboard than in a Christian home.

We could respond with a diatribe of indignation: "You're not going to talk like that in this household! How many times have we told you to clean up that mouth?" Or, for that matter, we could wash out their mouths with soap, but then they'd only resolve all the more to exert their independence. So our immediate response should be to move the problem out of earshot. Without anger, tell the child, "I'll be happy to talk to you when you can speak civilly to me and use clean and mature language."

When both we and our child have calmed down, we should talk about the problem itself. One approach is to address the child's sense of worth: "I think a lot of people who use that sort of language are people who don't feel all that good about themselves." Or we may want to take an intellectual tack: “Some people who use that sort of language have a very limited vocabulary. They don’t know many words, so they pull out those boring old swear words and use them. Nobody has to look them up in the dictionary. They’re really easy words. That’s probably why some people use them.” Then we should drop the issue. The language our children use will, in the long run, be the language they want to use. White-hot anger on our part will only delay their realization that immature people resort to such language.

Pearl 40

Teacher and School Problems

Generally, our role in our children's school life—in their grades and behavior—is to provide encouragement and good modeling. We leave the discipline to the teachers and administrators. We let our children handle their own school problems. But sometimes we may have to step in and approach a child's teacher. This is a difficult thing, for it often calls to mind all the feelings of intimidation we may have experienced with our own teachers.

When approaching a child's teacher, the attitude we should have is one of collecting information and thinking about it rather than storming into the teacher's room and offering solutions. We can make three common mistakes:

> ***Mistake One: We tell the teacher what to do.*** When we say, "I want my kid out of that classroom," what we are really telling the teacher is, "You aren't smart enough to figure out what to do, so I have to help you."
>
> ***Mistake Two: We go into the school with threats.*** Saying, "If I don't get my way, I'm going to go to the principal," creates even more problems than we had when we came in.
>
> ***Mistake Three: We muster an army of like-minded parents to assault the teacher en masse.*** Any victory in this sort of confrontation will be short-lived, for the teacher will fight for

his or her life. A variation of this tactic is saying, "I'm not the only person who's upset with this. A lot of others are too. But I'm the only one with the nerve to come talk to you."

All of these tactics are serious mistakes. We may have walked into the school with a problem, but when we leave, we'll have a problem and an enemy. In general, people who are put on the defensive are less inclined to come up with thoughtful solutions to problems.

Parents who get the best results with teachers are ones who use the magic word *describe.* It's magic because when we use it, we aren't *telling* the teacher anything. We're *describing* something: "I'd like to describe something that's happening and then give you my interpretation of it." When we've had our say, we can then use more magic words: "I'd like to get your thoughts on that." By saying this, we are telling the teacher we have confidence that she can think for herself.

Another approach is to ask, "What kind of options are available for solving a problem like this?" Then sit back and allow the teacher to think a while. Remember, as well as we think we know our children, we may not know how they react in a school environment. Frequently, children are a lot different at school than at home, so the teacher's interpretation of the situation is very helpful. A child who is easy to work with one-on-one may be frustrated and unruly when given one-twenty-fifth of that attention.

If we get no satisfaction with the teacher and want to kick the problem up the ladder, we should say, "Would you mind going with me to see if the principal has any thoughts on this?" That's a whole lot better than saying, "If I don't get my way, I'm going to the principal."

Our chief mission in approaching a teacher is to discuss our child's problem and see if a solution can be reached—to talk as well as listen, to suggest as well as take suggestions. Communication and respect for others are much more effective than commands and threats.

Pearl 41

Teeth Brushing

Kids, like the rest of us, love second chances. Those awful mistakes they make aren't nearly so haunting when they know there's another chance if they blow the first one.

One great opportunity for our children to have a second chance looks right at us every time they flash us their big, happy grins. In fact, there are twenty second chances staring at us—their baby teeth. Children are given a whole mouthful to practice their brushing techniques on, and when they've done that for eleven or twelve years, they're given a brand-new set. Getting kids to appreciate that opportunity can be a hassle though. They grab their brush and tube after every meal with about the same relish as we grab our calculator and tax forms every April. One little swipe across the pearly whites with the bristles, and they're ready to get on with living.

We can allow our kids to get in on the ground floor of conscientious dental hygiene and take the hassle out of the process all at the same time, but we have to be good models. Letting them see us brushing our teeth is effective, as is saying something like, "I just finished eating, and I think I'd better go protect my teeth with a little brushing."

Talking to our spouse is even more effective. One dad ended every meal by saying to his wife, "I sure can't go through the rest of the day with all that sugar on my teeth and in my mouth. I'd better go take care of it so I won't have cavities." He would then trot to the bathroom for a thorough brushing. When he returned, he would say to his wife, "I'm sure glad I did that. It took only a couple of minutes to get the job done, and I feel a whole lot better." Kids can thus follow what we say as well as how we feel after we've done it.

None of these kinds of comments can be too transparent for our eavesdropping children. They feel the excitement of overhearing something they think they shouldn't be hearing, and they're much more likely to try it themselves than if we get in their faces about it. However, as the "thrill" of brushing wears off, we may feel it necessary to get results by linking our kids' dental hygiene with things they want to do. Here, thinking words are the way to go: "You're welcome to go out to play as soon as your teeth are brushed," or "Feel free to watch television as soon as you brush your teeth."

One mom, before passing out cookies, prefaced the distribution with these words: "I pass out things with sugar in them to the people in this family who protect their teeth with brushing." Then she read roll call: "Noelle's been brushing her teeth, and Makayla's been brushing hers, and Claudia . . . well, Claudia, we'd better hold off on cookies until I don't have to worry so much about your teeth."

Claudia was a regular at the sink from that day on.

Pearl 42

Telephone Interruptions

Young children just don't understand telephone etiquette. Why, they are even capable of choosing the exact time when we are on the phone to ask us a question, hit us with a request, or otherwise seek our attention. Although technology has changed, you still can't talk to two different people about two different things at the same time. What usually happens is that the person on the other end of the line hears something like this: "Yes, Mr. Bosseroo, the Castleman report specifically stated—Taylor! Quit pulling on my pants!—Sorry about that, sir, but the numbers for the second quarter are in an obvious up—Taylor! Not now!" And Mr. Bosseroo thinks, *Why doesn't this guy get control of his kid?*

The fact is, we are not chained to that telephone. We can put it down. When we deal in a rational way with the problem of children interrupting, it permits our callers to abandon the notion that our domestic life resembles the halls of a junior high at day's end. If we handle our insistent children in a businesslike way—"Mr. Bosseroo, it looks like something has come up. Can you hang on for a second?"—our caller will not think less of us. Then get down on the child's level and briefly address him or her: "Taylor, honey, you need to run up to your room for five minutes. When five minutes are up, I want to see you down here again but with your mouth closed if I'm still on the telephone."

If Taylor refuses, then we must deal with the problem more extensively. Saying to our caller, "Can I call you right back?" will give us that opportunity. Callers usually accept this technique. They can see that we are taking control of our children and not allowing them to control us.

Plus, it's a lot more pleasant for them not having a human air-raid siren howling in the background.

Then sometime when the phone is not ringing (is there such a time?), we can pull our child onto our lap and hash it out:

DAD: "Taylor, honey, I notice that whenever I'm talking on the phone, you want to talk to me at the same time. Do you have any thoughts on that?"

TAYLOR: "I wanted to show you Cinderella and the wicked sisters. See?"

DAD: "Yes, Taylor. Let me look at it for a minute. . . . That's very pretty coloring. But I can do only one thing at a time, dear. When I'm talking on the phone, I can look at your Cinderella and the wicked sisters only a little. But when I'm not on the phone, I can look at them a lot."

TAYLOR: "But I wanted you to look at them when you were on the phone!"

DAD: "Well, I'm thinking that I can look at them a lot better when I'm not talking on the telephone. I really would like to look at them a lot, but I can't then because I have to talk to the person on the telephone. If you can show me your coloring when I can look a little or when I can look a lot, which do you think would be better?"

TAYLOR: "When you can look at them a lot."

DAD: "Right. And when would that be?"

TAYLOR: "When you're not talking on the phone."

This technique is also effective with kids who interrupt discussions between parents or between a parent and another adult. The message given to the child is that the interruptions are a problem and we don't like it. When it happens, the child must go somewhere else and think about it.

One parent reported that her strong-willed child didn't respond well to this method, so she engineered a training situation. She had one of her friends call and play along. When the child interrupted, Mom calmly said, "I'm sorry, Dawn. We have a little situation here." Calmly putting down the phone, she used the "Uh-Oh!" song technique. Her little one was whisked off to her room. "I'll see you when my phone call is over, sweetie." Mom was prepared to repeat this training session several times if necessary but found that one calm intervention did the trick.

Pearl 43

Television Watching

Every new media-use study brings on another bout of parental anxiety. The headlines are alarming: "Average child watches five hours of television a day, study says," or "Experts claim television dominant influence in average American kids' lives." We read the reports, cast a wary eye toward our kids imitating potted plants in front of the tube, and shake our heads in dismay. Television watching—What programs? How much time? When?—is the source of many parent-child tiffs. We are forever devising strategies to curtail our kids' television habits.

Many parents allow their young children hours in front of the TV, believing that at least preventing or discouraging the watching of sex and violence is adequate. However, we are more concerned about the fact *that* young children watch TV than *what* they watch. We are especially concerned about the amount of TV children watch before age six. When a child is between ages three and six, his or her brain is developing rapidly. These years, before the child learns to balance a bike, are important "learn-by-doing" years.

We strongly believe that hours of TV watching in toddlerhood and early childhood negatively impacts children's brain development and their later ability to focus on tasks. TV watchers often lack the ability to follow through on tasks in school. Their fragmentation on task completion may lead to a diagnosis of Attention Deficit Hyperactivity Disorder (ADHD). This is a misnomer and simply confuses the situation, for many of these children have no problem at all *attending*. In fact, a teacher may provide a videotape to "calm down the class." Indeed, these "ADHD" children have no problem at all attending to a clown, a magic act, videotapes, or games. Their problem occurs when the teacher asks them to focus on a task. With many, it's not an *attention* problem at all—it's an *intention* problem!

Whether watching a Disney video or a cartoon, children are spending valuable time learning to only attend, not focus on tasks and doing. We have found bored children to usually simply ask, "What can I *watch*?" instead of "What can I *do*?" just as their parents, who during their own formative years grew up with TV now turn on the tube to help them relax. As children grow older, wise parents, as we are about to note, avoid a control battle around TV watching. As with many other issues, modeling is the key.

It's pretty unreasonable for major league couch potatoes, who hit the "on" button at the opening theme of *Good Morning America* and the "off" button after the last joke on the *Late Show with David Letterman*, to come down hard on their children's television habits. That we must be aware of our own viewing habits is fairly obvious, but there's more. If we are more interesting to our children than the stuff that comes over the tube, they will prefer being with us. A simple "What do you say we go make that birdhouse, David," or "Okay, Claire, are you ready to take on your mom at Chinese checkers?" or "Come on out in the driveway, Christopher, and I'll show you the fine points of my world-famous sky hook" often will pry our kids away from the box. Most kids would much rather do something besides watch TV, as long as it's with someone they love. To influence our kids' television habits, we must emphasize the alternatives, playing up the good things about friends, family, hobbies, sports, and so on.

It's best not to set ourselves up for a control battle over television watching with commands and threats. Harping on our kids constantly or imposing severe cuts in their viewing habits often leads to rebellion. What we *can* do, however, is influence our kids. A generous dose of humor does wonders. Pushing on their heads as they watch television and declaring, "Well, it's not too soft yet," sends them the message that too much television will turn their brains to oat bran.

Foster once reminisced, for the benefit of his son Jerry (who was eleven at the time), about a brain operation he had performed as a neurosurgeon: "I remember my last neurosurgery case. This guy came in who was a little spacey. We couldn't figure out what was wrong with him, as the X-rays didn't show much, so we put him on the table and anesthetized him and then performed some burr holes in his head. Guess what happened? His brains flowed out the holes like thin cottage cheese. We couldn't understand it. Then we checked his file again, and there it was, clear as day: This guy had watched TV four hours a day for the past six weeks." Jerry's eyes popped out like a pirate's telescope because he had been watching four hours of television a day for the past *six years*!

In the long run, our kids will likely decide not to watch too much television because *they* have found other things to do or they believe it's not good for them.

Pearl 44

Temper Tantrums

The good news is there's usually a little warning: the big ear-to-ear frown, the flushing of the face, the balled-up little fists. Sometimes the little lips twitch spasmodically like a sort of warm-up exercise. All of these preliminaries give us a few seconds to sprint for the earmuffs before the little mouth opens wide and fills the room with a scream that would run shivers up and down Stephen King's spine.

The temper tantrum. Every child has his or her own style. Some plop their fannies down on the floor in preparation, others latch on to our legs as if they were tree trunks in a windstorm, and others fall back on tradition: the pounding-fists-on-the-floor routine. It actually could be sort of humorous—if it were someone else's kid and we had suitable ear protection in place!

The bad news is that temper tantrums happen regardless of what we do. At one time or another, every kid throws one. Unfortunately, many parents approach these tantrums with fear and loathing. They try to do everything humanly possible to prevent them, even to the point of avoiding saying "no" to their tyke for fear that the little fellow will explode like Mount St. Helens.

Two things to remember about tantrums: One, any kid worth keeping will probably throw a fit from time to time. Only kids whose spirits have been broken don't fight to get their way. Two, kids will throw tantrums only as long as they work. Kids never seem to scream and pound the floor when they're alone in their room, but the show goes on when they have a captive audience.

Wise parents simply let tantrums happen. There's nothing we can do to stop them anyway. What we can do, however, is change the location. We don't change *that* it is happening; we change *where.*

"I give that tantrum a 7.5," one parent told his howling Hannah. "It's not world-class, but it's pretty good for a local girl. Now, where would you like to have that tantrum so it won't disturb my ears?"

"Wa-a-a-a-a!" Hannah screams, pounding her fists on the floor and kicking at the air.

"It's up to an 8.2 now. Would you like to have it in the basement or in your room?"

Hannah shrieks from by the refrigerator, on which she is banging her head to emphasize her point.

"Oh, this is definitely a basement tantrum, Hannah. Hang on—I'll open the door. By the way, do you want the light on or off?"

You get the idea. Give a few choices, and get the kid downwind of you. Nothing in the parenting almanac says we have to put up with abuse like that, so we remove the child from our presence. We allow him or her to return when the hurricane dies down to a light drizzle.

The last thing we want to do is lose our composure, screaming back at our kids or saying, "You just keep on screaming and I'll give you something to really scream about!" Handling temper tantrums requires parents with soft voices who don't even try to reason with their misbehaving child. The message we want to send is, "That behavior is okay for now as long as I don't have to see or hear it."

Some parents are concerned about children hurting themselves while throwing tantrums. These parents should childproof the room, removing all dangerous or valuable objects. However, extreme violence rarely will occur if the audience is removed. If the children do hurt themselves, however, drive the lesson home with sadness over their injury when the tantrum is over. (In families in which this is a severe problem, professional counseling may be advised.)

Pearl 45

Toilet Training

Brace yourselves for this one, folks: Toilet training is fun! "What?" you shriek. "All that hassle just getting kids onto the potty chair? Then when we get them there, you'd think they'd go, right? Think again. They sit there for a few seconds and then stand right up, declare, 'All done!' and head off to the corner of the living room and do their dirty work *there*. Then there's all that mess to clean up. Fun? It's about as much fun as toxic waste!"

Okay, okay, we lied. What we meant to say was, "Toilet training *can be* fun—for us and for our kids." But first, the facts:

- Some children are naturally easy to toilet train and really train themselves. Some children are very difficult to train.
- Children differ developmentally. Some are ready at age two, while others may not be ready until four and a half.
- It is essential to keep the atmosphere around toilet training fun and exciting—even gleeful.
- Because we have a vested interest in our kids' potty habits, it is all too easy to become negative and frustrated. We really do want them to go into the potty.

Keeping these facts in mind, we can approach toilet training not like it's some kind of torture we all must submit to several times a day but with an enthusiastic and happy attitude. If *we* consider it a chore, our kids will follow suit.

Bear in mind, there is an anatomical difference between boys and girls. What works for one, won't work for the other. Keri draws pictures for her little daughter Bethany while they talk:

KERI: "Look, here's the kitty going potty in the hole that she digs. Look how happy the kitten is!"

BETHANY: "Is she happy?"

KERI: "Oh, she's so happy she's putting it there. All animals are different. Now, here's a doggie. He likes to go on a tree. Boy, is he happy. You know what? I want to make myself happy, so I'm going to go into the bathroom right now and put my pee-pee in the potty. I feel so good when I do that!"

BETHANY: "Can I do it too?"

KERI: "Oh, that would be wonderful, but not until I get to do it first."

With boys we can get right down to a little first-person modeling action. Kevin plays "Sink the Bismarck" with his little son Alex:

KEVIN: "I take this toilet paper and I wad it up, Alex, and I throw it in there, and you know what that is?"

ALEX: "No."

KEVIN: "That's a PT boat. And here's another one, a battleship. Can you guess what I'm going to do, Alex?"

ALEX: "No."

KEVIN: "I'm going to sink them all. Watch!"

ALEX: "Can I do that too?"

KEVIN: "If you're a good shot. But you have to be quick because they sink by themselves pretty fast."

Some parents tape two lollipops to the bathroom door for post-duty enjoyment—not as a bribe but because kids and parents feel so good when they're done that they feel they both deserve them. One tactic to avoid, however, is the "You sit there until you go" routine. It can cause a lot of hard feelings and is usually ineffective.

Pearl 46

Values: Passing Them On to Your Kids

Every day it seems there's another story of the decline in values in our youth in the United States. Drugs are available in even remote rural schools. Teenage sexually transmitted infections are skyrocketing. In many schools, teachers are more police officers than they are instructors. A troubling materialism rears its ugly head even among elementary school students. In our society, proper moral values seem to be taking a pretty good licking. As parents, this disturbing trend brings the cold sweat of responsibility to our furrowed brows. "I want my children to have responsible moral values," we say, "but how do I teach them those values?"

Parents cannot make their kids think like they do simply by telling them, "You'll do it or else." Demands and threats may yield short-term results, but they don't mold our kids' minds. They don't persuade them that we're right. In a real sense, parenting is the transmitting of our values to our kids. We want our kids to be honest; we want them to respect others; we want them to know the value of hard work; we want a moral and ethical lifestyle to be as important to them as it is to us.

However, there's bad news and good news in this question of transmitting values. The bad news is that we can't stroll down the wide and easy road of lecturing our kids on the topic. It might have worked for our parents, but the odds for success have radically tipped the other way. The good news, though, is that it *is* still possible to pass on our values to our kids, but it's going to take some thought and effort.

Values are passed on to children in two ways: by what our kids *see* and by what they *experience in relating to us.* When our kids see us being honest, they learn about honesty. When we talk to our kids with love and respect, they learn to talk that way to others.

We can accelerate our modeling effectiveness by engaging in "eavesdrop value setting." That means that Mom and Dad talk to each other about their values but within earshot of the kids. If we want our children to learn about honesty, for example, we allow them to overhear us reporting on our genuine acts of honesty. "You know, sweetie," we might say to our spouse, "something interesting happened to me today. At the store, I gave the clerk a five-dollar bill for a can of pop, and she gave me $14.50 in change. So I gave her back the ten. I could have said nothing and been ten dollars richer, but I feel so much better being honest and doing what's right."

Or if our peers tell some off-color and demeaning stories at work, we may say to our spouse, when our kids can overhear us, "The guys at the office were telling dirty stories today in the lunchroom, but I excused myself and ate lunch at my desk. It always bothers me to hear stories like that. I feel much better for thinking for myself and walking away."

Kids soak up what they hear when we speak to others. It's great when what they soak up is good, but be advised: They're sponges for the bad too. Our improper words and actions hit them with the same force. If we have nothing but ridicule for our bosses and coworkers, our kids learn that ridicule and sarcasm are an acceptable way to talk. If we cheat at board games or when we play sports with our young children, then we shouldn't wring our hands and cry, "Why?" when they get nailed for cheating at school. If our idea of a good time is a La-Z-Boy recliner, a six-pack of beer, and an NFL doubleheader, our kids will get the message that that's the way grown-ups have fun. All of our wise words to the contrary won't blunt that point.

The other way we influence our kids' values is in the way we treat them. A corollary to the Golden Rule applies here: Kids will do to others as their parents do to them. Treating our kids with respect teaches them to go and do likewise. Being fair with our kids makes them want to be fair to their friends and teachers.

Kids have minds of their own. They want to exert their independence and do their own thinking. They blow off the things that are forced onto them and embrace the things they want to believe. If we want to pass our values down to them, we must present those values in a way our kids can accept: in our actions and words. Kids' values come from what they see and hear. They don't accept what we try to drive into their heads through lecturing.

Pearl 47

Video and Computer Games

Just as we are able to control the amount of time our children spend in front of the television, we can set time limits on the minutes or hours our children spend shooting bad guys or racing cars from behind their video-game console. Assuming that children are obedient, we can control the amount of time they spend playing video games inside our own home. The problem is, however, if we attempt to set such limits for our children *wherever* they may be, we risk getting into a control battle that we will certainly lose. Not only that, when *we* control the time our children spend playing video games, we are, in essence, saying, "You don't have the self-discipline to limit yourself." Such external limits, while sometimes necessary, discourage independent decision making and self-control. That's sad because both skills are essential when our children make choices regarding use of the car, friends, substance abuse, and sexual activity.

Because limits can always be resorted to within our homes, let's try other things first. Let's make sure our children have the opportunity to practice setting their own limits, ideally when the cost of making mistakes is low and they are dealing with video games rather than substance abuse or sex.

Let's listen in on a wise dad discussing video games with his son. He follows the Love and Logic steps always recommended when dealing with issues directly affecting the children:

1. Confirm that this is a good time for the conversation.

2. Show curiosity, interest, and acceptance (though not necessarily approval); use thoughtful questions to explore your child's point of view.
3. Ask if you can share your thoughts and observations.
4. Give your ideas succinctly and lovingly, without over-lecturing. Continue with questions if appropriate.
5. Thank your child for listening and close with the hope that he or she will consider your opinion.

DAD: (looking over his son's shoulder as blood of bad guys splatters across the screen) "Hey, Rob, looks like you're doing pretty well! How's it going?"

ROB: "Great, Dad! I'm on level four now, and I've wiped out a whole enemy platoon."

DAD: "I bet you feel great about that! How long have you been fighting here?"

ROB: "About half an hour so far today, and about two hours yesterday."

DAD: "Wow. Lot's of time fighting. What do you like best about playing?"

ROB: "Well, I like outsmarting the enemy. These new games are so realistic. Something that works the first time doesn't work the second. The bad guys learn! It's the artificial intelligence programming."

DAD: "Yeah, I can see how that's really exciting. Is it just you, or are you leading a platoon?"

ROB: "Both. Depends on how I set up the situation!"

DAD: "Interesting. . . . Do you mind pausing the action while we talk a minute?"

ROB: "Sure, Dad." (Kids tend to want to hear what their parents have to say when they are used to parents giving observations, ideas, and thoughts rather than orders, demands, and accusations.)

DAD: "You know, Rob, I have always thought of you as a person with real leadership qualities, and I always thought that you would make a difference in a world of your own creation and that other people would play by your rules."

ROB: "What do you mean, Dad?"

DAD: "Well, as exciting as the combat is, you are living in a world created by very talented and creative computer artists and coders. They've been really good at creating worlds where other people want to spend a lot of time."

ROB: "Yeah, but it's not like I'm not making my own decisions."

DAD: "I bet you make good ones. Can you make *any* decision?"

ROB: "No, not any."

DAD: "Right. You can't decide to climb a tree, right?"

ROB: "No."

DAD: "Or set up possibilities for peace."

ROB: "Dad, this game isn't about peace!"

DAD: "Well, that's kind of my point. It seems a little limiting to me. You get to advance to new levels in a way they have programmed, right?"

ROB: "Well, yeah, I guess."

DAD: "Don't get me wrong, Rob. When I see you here enjoying the game, I realize that most people play the game of life by other people's rules. So join the human race. However, the more time you spend outside of virtual reality, with real people, the more you gain skills to communicate and create a world of *your* own making, not someone else's."

ROB: "I get your drift, Dad."

DAD: "Well, good luck, pal! Thanks for giving this some thought."

Video Game Addiction

Problems with video games can go much deeper than this, and dealing with them can have many of the same challenges as facing up to any other addiction, such as gambling. The following story can give us an example, and hope, about such situations:

"How could this happen?" worried Jared's mother. She finally realized that her son had become addicted to Internet computer games. Before today, she had been ambivalent about the amount of time he spent in his room playing the games and was able to convince herself that it was not all that bad. After all, when he is off in his room, they aren't arguing about things and he's not underfoot.

Denial has great power over humans. In this case, it helped Mom avoid seeing the real problem. She even had days when she was able to think, *Other kids are out smoking dope. Other kids are out getting into trouble. How can his interest in the games be so bad? He's safe in his room; I know where he is and what he's doing.* Of course, this kind of thinking makes about as much sense as, *Other kids rape and murder. My kid's not that bad. He only sells drugs.*

Recently, she'd seen a television news show that touted the millions of dollars a local school paid to provide academic instruction through computer games. The news reporter said the kids loved the games and were actually scoring better on their school tests. This information helped her feel better about Jared's compulsive use of the computer games at home.

Jared's mom actually convinced herself that all the time he spent on the computer games was good for his self-concept. She told her friend Bridget, "You know, Jared isn't good at a lot of things other boys are good at. Now he's found something that he's good at. I just know that his self-concept will grow with his success at the games."

But alas, Mom's thinking got a jolt. She attended a seminar on addictions. The expert talked about common addictions, such as alcohol, drugs, and gambling. It was a shock when the therapist talked about the devastating effects of computer addiction. She learned about the breakdown of family relationships when children or adults become consumed with their computers and lose interest in each other. Depression increases in many of these families as well. Adding to her concern, she learned about documented changes in the brain experienced by those who become addicted to the games.

Mom developed new resolve to look at what she had done to her son by encouraging his infatuation with the screen and the keyboard. She realized that family members had drifted apart since she had allowed the computer to take over raising her children.

Mom now knew she had to take action. She and Dad sought out the services of an addiction specialist in an attempt to understand the challenges they and their son were going to face. The therapist helped them understand they would soon be seeing typical behaviors of addicts.

"No," said Mom. "Jared is a good kid who has never been prone to being sneaky or defiant. He will understand that we are trying to help him." Months later, she told how wrong she was about this. "When we took away his computer, he sneaked time on his dad's computer. When we put a password on Dad's computer, he found a way to break the password. He told us he was going to his friend's home to do homework, but instead he used his friend's machine to continue his gaming."

Jared even found a way to buy a used computer, which he hid in his room. Mom and Dad never discovered where he got the money to buy it. They were equally surprised to learn he would sneak away to the Cyber Café when he was supposed to be in school. Truancy became a major problem.

Like all similar situations, this problem got worse before it started to turn around. Fortunately, with the support of a therapist and due to Jared's determination to rejoin the real world instead of the fantasy world of gaming, there was a happy ending to this story.

As this mom looked back on this problem and how it consumed her family, she related her disappointment that she didn't learn about Love and Logic when her children were younger. "I'm sure the fantasy world of the games had a lot to do with the fact that they provided an illusion of control for a boy who had too few choices and consequences in his real life. He was denied the opportunity to feel needed in our family. This happened when we gave up on trying to get him to do his fair share of the work around the house. The reason we gave up was because we didn't know how to get him to do chores without constant reminders and battles. I now know that Jared has an addictive personality that made it easy to slip into the gaming addiction as a way of replacing what he was not getting out of his family life. I'm sure the odds of avoiding this problem would have been much higher had we known and used the Love and Logic process as we raised him."

In summary, the issue of video games sometimes puts parents between a rock and a hard spot. On the one hand, we want our kids to make their own choices (for example, how much time they spend playing video games). On the other hand, if they cannot make the correct choices, an addiction could develop. The Love and Logic approach is to allow children to make their own decisions unless their health is endangered. Love and Logic parents encourage and counsel, just as would a good therapist. However, with a true addiction, in which functioning is at risk, the control battle may be worth the hassle. Certainly, though, many parents handle the issue the simple way: From the time the children are young, they simply do not *have* video games in the home. We applaud those folks!

Pearl 48

Whining and Complaining

It's ten o'clock in the morning, and Nolan wants a cookie. He knows he can't have one, but that has never stopped him from asking before, and it won't stop him now. "Mommy, I want a cookie," he whines, his little fingers clutching the seam on his mom's jeans.

"Nolan, you know you can't have cookies between meals," Mom returns. "Now, run off and play."

"But Mommy, I want one," Nolan continues.

"You can have one at lunchtime. Now, off you go."

"I don't want to wait. I want one *now*."

"Well, you can't have one."

"But, Mom-m-my. I want one *now-w-w*!"

Then it happens. Parents who tolerate whining from their kids eventually whine back. "Will you stop *whin-ing*?" Mom says. "I *hate* it when you whine like that!"

No wonder Nolan whines like a pro: He has a good teacher. The fact is, parents who spend a lot of time pleading with their children develop kids who are experts at pleading. Quite often, just to get rid of that long-playing, sing-songy record of complaint, we surrender and grudgingly fork over the cookie. The message the child gets is that whining works.

Some schoolteachers effectively fight whining with multiple-choice questions. Jim once heard a teacher say, "Do you suppose I'll be able to understand you better when you're whining or not whining? Why don't you go to your desk and think about that? Come back when you've decided."

We can do the same. Saying, "When your voice sounds like mine, I'll be glad to talk with you," addresses the real problem with whining: the child's tone of voice. Whether or not Nolan can have a cookie will be discussed later, after the syrupy, high-pitched pleading stops. However, kids are nothing if not persistent. Sometimes saying, "I won't listen to you while you're whining," encourages them and provides the emotional feedback they want. By saying it, we may actually be responding to their whining. What then?

If we think we aren't getting results by asking our whining children to leave or if we find ourselves drawn into a discussion, then we can win the battle by ignoring the whining altogether. It is best, however, to explain this method before employing it. Sit the child down when emotions are calm and say, "Nolan, if Dad and I ever act like we don't hear you, it's not because we don't hear you. We do. It's just that we don't want to hear you unless you talk a certain way. That's why we won't answer your question. But when you can talk nicely, in the same tone of voice we talk in, then you'll get an answer." Eventually, kids will realize that we'll listen only when they're speaking nicely.

Appendix A—The Three Types of Parents

Helicopter	Drill Sergeant	Consultant
This parent hovers over their children and rescues them from the hostile world in which they live.	*This parent commands and directs the lives of their children.*	*This Love and Logic parent provides guidance and consultant services for their children.*
1. Provides messages of weakness and low personal worth	1. Provides messages of low personal worth and resistance	1. Provides messages of personal worth and strength
2. Makes excuses for the child but complains about mishandled responsibilities	2. Makes many demands and has lots of expectations about responsibility	2. Very seldom mentions responsibilities
3. Takes on the responsibility of the child	3. Tells the child how he or she should handle responsibility	3. Demonstrates how to take care of self and responsibilities
4. Protects the child from any possible negative feelings	4. Tells the child how he or she should feel	4. Shares personal feelings about own performance and responsibilities
5. Makes decisions for the child	5. Provides absolutes: "This is the decision you should make!"	5. Provides and helps explore alternatives and then allows child to make his or her own decision
6. Provides no structure but complains, "After all I've done for you . . . "	6. Demands that jobs or responsibilities be done now	6. Provides time frames in which child may complete responsibilities
7. Whines and uses guilt: "When are you ever going to learn? I always have to clean up after you."	7. Issues orders and threats: "You get that room cleaned up or else . . . "	7. Models doing a good job, finishing, cleaning up, and feeling good about it
8. Whines and complains about having an irresponsible child who causes "me" much work and responsibility	8. Takes over ownership of the problem using threats and orders to solve the problem	8. Makes sure the child owns the problem; helps the child explore solutions to his or her own problem
9. Uses many words and actions that indicate that the child is not capable or responsible	9. Uses many harsh words, very few actions	9. Uses many actions but very few words
10. Protects child from natural consequences; uses guilt as the teacher	10. Uses punishment; pain and humiliation serve as the teacher	10. Allows child to experience life's natural consequences

Appendix B — Turn Your Word into Gold: The Art of Enforceable Statements for the Home

Ineffective Technique	Love and Logic Technique
Please sit down. We're going to eat now.	We will eat as soon as you are seated.
Please be quiet. I can't listen to your brother when you are both talking at the same time.	I'll be glad to listen to you as soon as your brother has finished talking to me.
Clean your room so we can go shopping.	I'll be happy to take you shopping as soon as your room is clean.
I'm not going to play ball with you until you are quiet.	I'll be happy to play ball with you as soon as you are quiet.
Don't talk while I'm reading to you.	I will start reading to you again as soon as you have finished talking.
You can't go play until you have finished your homework.	Feel free to go play as soon as you have finished your homework.
Don't shout at me.	I listen to people who do not yell at me.
Pay attention.	I'll start again as soon as I know you are with me.
Don't bother your sister.	You are welcome to stay with us as long as you are not bothering your sister.
Keep your hands to yourself.	Feel free to hang out with us when you can keep your hands to yourself.
Do your chores on time or you'll be grounded.	I'll be happy to let you go with your friends as soon as your chores are finished.
Don't talk to me in that tone of voice!	I'll listen as soon as your voice is as calm as mine.
You show some respect.	I'll be glad to discuss this when respect is shown.

Don't be late coming home from school.	I drive to practice those who arrive home on time.
I'm not picking up your dirty clothes.	I'll be glad to wash the clothes that are put in the laundry room.
Keep your room neat.	All keepers of neat rooms are welcome to join us for ice cream.
I'm not loaning you any more money.	I lend money to those who have collateral.
If you can't remember your pencil, you're just going to have to do without.	Feel free to borrow from anyone but me.
You're not going out without your coat.	You may go out as soon as you have your coat.
You're not going to stay in this group and act like that.	You may stay with us if you can give up that behavior.
Don't you come back to this room until you can show some respect!	Feel free to come back to the room as soon as you are calm.
Quit breaking the rules of the game.	Those who can follow the rules are welcome to continue playing the game.
Get this room cleaned up right now, and I mean it!	You may join us for ice cream sundaes as soon as your room is clean.
Stop arguing with me.	I'll be glad to discuss this with you as soon as your arguing stops.
If you can't treat the paintbrushes right, you'll just have to sit out this project.	All of those who can handle the paintbrushes right are welcome to join us on the project.
If you forget your permission slip, you're going to miss the field trip.	All of those who remember permission slips are welcome to go on the field trip.

Notes

1. For more on being a consultant parent to adolescents, see our book *Parenting Teens with Love and Logic.*

2. For more on the three different parenting types, see appendix A.

3. Many specific problems are discussed in part 2, "Love and Logic Parenting Pearls."

4. For more examples of this, see appendix A.

5. Sylvia B. Rimm, PhD, *How to Parent So Children Will Learn* (Watertown, WI.: Apple Publishing, 1990).

6. More on these specific issues in part 2.

7. Also see Pearl 46, "Values: Passing Them On to Your Kids."

8. For more information and advice on this topic, see *From Innocence to Entitlement* from the Love and Logic Institute. Available at www.loveandlogic.com. In Love and Logic tradition, the book offers specific and practical techniques for parents to combat childhood entitlement.

9. For more information and advice on this topic, see *Grandparenting with Love and Logic* from the Love and Logic Institute. Available at www.loveandlogic.com.

10. www.livescience.com, August 2005.

11. Peter Cary, "Fixing Kids' Sports," *U.S. News & World Report*, vol. 136, no. 20 (June 7, 2004): 46-47.

Index

Authors

Foster Cline, MD, is an internationally renowned child and adult psychiatrist. He is a cofounder, with Jim Fay, of the Love and Logic Institute and specializes in the attachment and bonding of children, dealing with gifted and talented children, parenting and child management, classroom behavior management, and communications systems and patterns.

His love of children and his passion for changing lives give him a unique sense of clarity as he turns difficult and often confusing child development concepts into straight talk and answers for adults. He has served as a consultant to school systems, pupil personnel teams, and hospitals around the world.

Dr. Cline is also a grandparent and the father of three biological children, one adopted child, and several foster children.

Jim Fay has more than fifty years of experience working with children and families. During thirty-one years in education as an educator, principal, and administrator, he served in public, private, and parochial schools. He is a cofounder of the Love and Logic Institute as well as the founder of School Consultant Services, which he began in 1977.

Fay has become one of America's most sought-after presenters in the field of parenting, positive discipline, and classroom management. He has been a consultant to schools, parents, mental health organizations, and the U.S. military. He is also recognized as one of America's top educational experts and has won many awards in the education field.

Fay is a grandparent and the father of three children. His youngest, Charles Fay, PhD, is a school psychologist and has joined the Love and Logic Institute as a presenter, writer, and consultant.

Love and Logic Materials and Seminars

Foster Cline, MD, and Jim Fay present Love and Logic seminars for both parents and educators in many cities each year. For more information on their books, CDs, seminars, or other helpful materials, contact:

The Love and Logic Institute, Inc.
2207 Jackson St., Suite 102
Golden, Colorado 80401-2300
(800) LUV-LOGIC
(800) 588-5644
(303) 278-7552
Fax: (800) 455-7557

Or visit our website at:
www.loveandlogic.com